Thou Art Mine

Thou Art Mine

Lance Lambert

LANCE LAMBERT MINISTRIES
Richmond, VA

ISBN 978-1-68389-071-3
www.lancelambert.org

Contents

Preface

The following messages were presented by Lance Lambert at the Christian Family Conference held in Richmond, Virginia during July 1986. His spoken words have been transcribed into this book and edited only for clarity.

And His voice shook the earth then, but now He has promised, saying, "Yet once more I will shake not only the Earth, but also the heaven." (Hebrews 12:26 New American Standard)

Considering the hour in which we live there is much uncertainty and insecurity throughout the whole world. Thankfully, God's people do not have to look to the world for security. Through three little words found in Isaiah 43:1, "Thou Art Mine" Lance Lambert reminds us that there is tremendous security in the fact that, if we are the Lord's people, we belong to Him. He shares that there are four ways in which the Lord claims us as His own. We are His by creation, we are His by redemption, we are His by calling, and we are His through overcoming.

Although it is true that the Lord is ours, it is vital that we know in our hearts that we are the Lord's—to know that He says, "THOU ART MINE." Our security is in the Lord Jesus.

1.
Thou Art Mine By Creation

Isaiah 43:1–2

But now thus saith the Lord that created thee, O Jacob, and he that formed thee, O Israel: Fear not, for I have redeemed thee; I have called thee by thy name, thou art mine. When thou passest through the waters, I will be with thee; and through the rivers, they shall not overflow thee: when thou walkest through the fire, thou shalt not be burned, neither shall the flame kindle upon thee.

Shall we pray:

Dear Heavenly Father, we are so glad that we have been able, by the power of your Holy Spirit, to open up our hearts to You in worship and praise. And now Lord, as we come to Your word, we want to confess our absolute dependence upon You, both for speaking and for hearing. Unless You are that ability, that anointing, then Lord, my speaking and our hearing will all be in vain. But Lord,

You are the One who not only brings to birth in our hearts a word, but You are the One who gives the anointing by which that word can be communicated to others. You are the One who gives the anointing so that we hear what You are saying in that word and are doers of it. Lord, we just give ourselves to You. Hedge us in with Yourself, and we pray that You will make the ministry of the word very precious to every one of us. We ask it in the name of our Lord, Jesus. Amen.

These well-known words of Isaiah have been in my heart for over two years and two or three times I thought the time had come to share them, but each time the Lord thought differently. I had all the meditation and reflection, and on one occasion it came right to the actual time, but at the last moment the Lord gave me another word altogether and took us into a quite different direction. Now, there seems to be some reason why the Lord wants this shared. Then I think to myself, "Well, what is the point of bringing this kind of word to all the folks here? They all know this anyway; it is so simple. It is not one of those great mysteries about the body, or the testimony of Jesus, or the book of Revelation." Yet, there has to be some reason why the Lord wants this particular word shared at this particular time.

I suppose all of you know this passage, even those of you who hardly ever read the Old Testament. This is one of those passages, along with Psalm 23, which all believers know. The key to this marvelous statement of the Lord's is in three words, "Thou art mine." It is not the rivers that we have to go through, the waters that are not going to overflow us, the fire that we might pass through, or the flame that will not kindle upon us. It is this incredible statement by God Himself concerning you and me: "Thou art mine." And we cannot get out of it. If He had only left Jacob out of the picture, a lot of us could have felt, "Well, He is not talking about me. He is talking about very elite saints, those people who never think an evil thought and never do an evil thing. They are His." But it is to Jacob that He addresses these words: "But now thus saith the Lord that created thee, O Jacob, and He that formed thee, O Israel: Fear not, for I have redeemed thee; I have called thee by thy name, thou (Jacob) art mine. When thou passeth through the waters, I will be with thee; and through the rivers, they shall not overflow thee: when thou walkest through the fire, thou shalt not be burned, neither shall the flame kindle upon thee."

There is a tremendous security in the fact that we belong to Him. Most of Christianity tends to put the emphasis on the fact that He is mine. And, of course, that is absolutely true. If you are a child of God, the Lord Jesus is yours. All the fathomless, unsearchable riches of God in Christ, all the infinite fulness and power of the Godhead in Christ, every spiritual blessing in heavenly places in Christ that you have been blessed with, is all yours. God will supply every single need of yours according to His riches in glory in Christ Jesus. The Lord Jesus belongs to you, and it is true as the old hymn says in its chorus, "Mine, mine, mine." But it seems to me that is where Christianity has tended to put the whole emphasis: "Mine, mine, mine; He is mine." I am so glad that the Lord says here, "Thou art mine." I find a tremendous security there.

Of course, when you are young, you do not think so much about this because you feel you have a bit more strength and power. So you think, "Well, I am going to hold on to Him. Whatever comes

I am going to hold on to Him; He is mine. He is the unspeakable gift of God to me. I am going to hold on to Him." But when you get a little older, and have been knocked about a bit more, and you have gone through a few more experiences, you come to the place where you almost wonder whether you can hold on to Him. Sometimes it seems as if the clouds and the storm obscure Him altogether, and then you wonder whether you have lost Him. What a security there is in knowing, "I am His." Whatever storm comes, He is never going to loosen His hold on me. Divine love has taken hold of you and has taken hold of me, and He is not likely to let go. No one is going to pluck you out of His hand; you are His.

I am so glad that my salvation does not finally rest on the decision I made concerning Him. I would be very afraid if my salvation really rested on my choice of Him. I remember those words—mysterious, fathomless and absolutely accurate, although beyond my understanding—"You did not choose Me, but I chose you." Some people get terribly worked up about this because they think, "Oh dear, he is not going to introduce Calvinism into this time, is he? Surely there is such a thing as human responsibility."

I have no doubt that there is such a thing as human responsibility, and I have no problem about preaching the gospel and demanding some kind of decision on the part of those who hear. But I have to say that in some mysterious way, beyond my little finite mind, I discover that the Lord chose me. How it all works out, I do not know, and whether I shall ever understand it, I do not even know. But in some way, as far as I can see, the Lord chose me and chose you. You are His, as He says in this word, "Thou art mine."

I think of another word in Malachi 3:17a: "And they shall be mine, saith the Lord of hosts, even mine own possession, in the day that I make."

I think of the words of the Apostle Peter in 1 Peter 2:9–10: "But ye are an elect race, a royal priesthood, a holy nation, a people for God's own possession, that ye may show forth the excellencies of him who called you out of darkness into his marvelous light: who in time past were no people, but now are the people of God: who had not obtained mercy, but now have obtained mercy."

In this wonderful statement that the Lord made in Isaiah 43, I see four ways in which we are His. First, we are His by creation: "But now thus saith the Lord that created thee, O Jacob." Secondly, we are His by redemption: "That formed thee, O Israel: Fear not, for I have redeemed thee." Thirdly, we are His by calling: "I have called thee by name, thou art mine." And fourthly, we are His by overcoming: "Though thou passeth through the rivers they shall not overflow thee."

The first way that we see we are His is by creation. This may sound very simple, and it may seem to many of you who are older in the Lord that it does not really have anything to do with you. But it has a tremendous amount to do with every single one of us because God claims Jacob by creation as well as by redemption. When we think about it, it brings us to one or two quite simple but foundational truths. God's claim on Jacob is that He created him: "But now thus saith the Lord that created thee, O Jacob." God foreknew Jacob. There was not a single facet of his twisted character that God had not foreseen and foreknown. His whole genetic history was under the sovereign government of God. God was not only behind the kind of genes that made up the temperament and personality of Jacob, but He was the One who knew the depths to which Jacob could stoop. This was God's claim on him: "I have created you, O Jacob."

God's dealings with you began long before you were converted. If you think that God only started with you on the day you were converted, on the day you were born again, you really do not understand your salvation. Actually, God's dealings with you as a person go back before your natural birth. When you were in your mother's womb, the Lord knew you. Long before you ever came on the scene, the Lord knew every single thing there was to know about you—all your pedigree, all your genealogy. You do not even know your genealogy. Most of us do not know. We might go back to our great grandparents or even our great-great grandparents, but how many of us really know the whole family tree? And yet, God has foreknown you and has watched over your genetic history. You are not a coincidence; you are not a mistake; you are not just some little bit of debris on a human lake that God saved and then got interested in. God knew you from before the foundation of the world. He knew everything that was to make you a unique personality in His sight. And though you may have been born into a fallen world with a fallen nature and a self-centered constitution, still God was behind everything that you are today. He was not the author of your sin, but He is behind everything to do with you.

That is what I find in those amazing words, "Jacob, have I loved." If He had only said, "Israel have I loved," many Christians would have been more comfortable. They would have said, "Well, of course the Lord loved Israel because the Lord only loves the saint. Once He got him to the place where He wanted him to be, He loved him." But the interesting thing is that God does not say, "Israel I have loved." He could have said that; but He said, "Jacob have I loved." Again and again in the Bible, God is known as "the God of Jacob." It is as if God wants us to know that He can save and love the lowest single denominator in human character. I find this tremendous! So I come back to this word, "But now thus saith the Lord that created thee, O Jacob."

The Distinctive Nature of Man

Some Christians have a terrible argument with their personality. Some people who are rather cautious or retiring by nature feel that they should be out-going exhibitionists. Those who are very extrovert in nature have a terrible battle with themselves and feel they should be very cautious and restrained. Those who are by nature colorful and vivid people feel they should be drab and colorless. They have a kind of sneaking suspicion that they should be little worms that crawl around on the earth. And those who are by nature very quiet and very low-lying people feel they should be more definite and more "out on top." So there develops within us a kind of battle with ourselves. Actually, we end up having an argument with God: "Why have you made me so?" That is really what it comes down to. Of course we would not say that. We say, "The Lord does not like this." But God knows your genetic history, and the personality and temperament you have is all part of His plan—not the sin, not the fall, not the self-centeredness.

When you and I come to a very simple recognition that He created us, we start to go places with God. Otherwise, we fall into the trap where we are all the time projecting a kind of artificial image concerning ourselves. We believe we should be this, but God does not want us to be this. God has made us in a different way. Sometimes I go into meetings where everyone has modeled himself or herself to a particular brother or sister. They all pray like them. It is a kind of feeling we have within ourselves: "That is what I ought to be like." But Jacob was Jacob, and Isaac was Isaac, and Abraham was Abraham, and Joseph was Joseph, and Moses was Moses, and Joshua was Joshua, and David was David. Isn't it so?

When we come to the New Testament, you may have a Matthew, a Mark, a Luke, and a John, but every one of them is distinctive, and their personality comes through even in the way that they present the story and history of Jesus. Why didn't the Lord steamroller the whole thing out and reveal Himself as one kind of personality in all thought? But He did not do this. He is so great that He needs a Matthew, He needs a Mark, He needs a Luke, and He needs a John to reveal this fourfold greatness of the Lord Jesus.

When you come to the letters of the New Testament, you do not have to study your New Testament for very long to be able to tell the difference between the style of John the apostle, the style of Paul the apostle, and the style of James. Or am I being stupid? Are they all the same? Paul says things that James would never dream of saying; yet James is as inspired by the Holy Spirit as Paul. Paul says, "You are justified apart from works." And James says, "You are justified by works, as well as faith." Actually, they are saying the same thing. James is saying, "You do not have faith unless it works," and Paul is saying, "If you think you can do good works instead of faith and get saved, you are in a false way." And then John never did see any in between. He was always either black or white. Wouldn't you have thought that if the Holy Spirit really got into these men, He would have steamrollered out all these little eccentricities of their personalities and styles? Then we would have one common style in which you would not be able to tell the difference between John and Paul, or John and Paul from James. But no, they are all quite distinctive.

That is why this matter is of such importance to you and to me. If the enemy can push us into a false battle over our personality and our temperament, he has won a very big position because we start to project a false image of what we think God wants us to be. In the end, we end up with a projected image that everybody sees, but the real you and me is trapped in a dungeon inside and never sees the light of day spiritually. We see that our real self is locked up down underneath somewhere. How is the Lord going to conform you and me to the image of His Son when He cannot even get to us, when all He can get of us is a projected image?

It is Jacob that God created. And when God took hold of Jacob, He was not saying to him, "I want you to be Isaac." He did not say to Jacob, "I want you to be Abraham." He did not say to Jacob, "I want you to be Moses." Even when Jacob became Israel, it was still his own personality and temperament that was filled with the Holy Spirit and then broken through the work of the cross. The beauty of the Lord was upon him.

God's Original Design in Creation

What was God's original design in creation? When God first created man and breathed into him, man became a living soul.

God created you and me as tripartite beings. There is not a human being without a spirit, a soul, and a body. Angels are spirits who do not have bodies like you and me. Animals also have a kind of soul, but it is not eternal. Anyone who knows anything about animals knows they have personalities. Two dogs are not the same; two cats are not the same. I understand, though I have never gone into it deeply, that even two fish are not the same. Those who catch fish tell me that even fish have personality, relatively speaking. But man was quite unique because man is the only being created by God that has three parts to his being—spirit, soul, and body.

And the God of peace himself sanctify you wholly;
and may your spirit and soul and body be
preserved entire, without blame at the coming of
our Lord Jesus Christ. 1 Thessalonians 5:23

I do not understand why so many theological seminaries teach that man is bipartite; that is, he has only soul and body, and the spirit is merely another name for the soul. They say the spirit is the spiritual side of the inward man, and the soul is the more emotional side of the inward man. Why then does Paul, by the Spirit of God, say that your whole being may be preserved entire— your spirit, soul, and body?

Then again, in Hebrews 4:12 we read:

For the word of God is living, and active, and
sharper than any two-edged sword, and piercing
even to the dividing of soul and spirit.

Now what does that mean, if the spirit is another word for the soul and the soul another word for the spirit? Why does it speak of the word of God dividing between soul and spirit, unless the soul and the spirit have quite distinct functions?

Nor is it confined only to the New Testament. In the Old Testament we have the intimation of it, for instance, in Psalm 131:1–3:

> *Lord, my heart is not haughty, nor mine eyes lofty;*
> *neither do I exercise myself in great matters, or in*
> *things too wonderful for me. Surely I have stilled and*
> *quieted my soul; like a weaned child with his mother,*
> *like a weaned child is my soul within me. O Israel, hope*
> *in the Lord from this time forth and for evermore.*

Who is doing the weaning? "I have weaned my soul within me; I have stilled my soul within me like a weaned child." Does that mean my body is stilling my soul? That is strange if this old flesh is getting hold of my emotions and saying, "Shut up." It seems to me there is an intimation here that it is the spirit of the man within him, and this spirit is taking authority over his own soul and saying, "Shoosh."

"Be still my soul." Who is talking to whom? It cannot be his soul talking to his soul, can it? Then is it his body talking to his soul? It must be his spirit that is talking to his soul and saying, "Be still my soul."

I think of another one in Psalm 103:1:

Bless the Lord, O my soul; and all that is
within me, bless his holy name.

Who is talking to whom? It must be the spirit of the psalmist that has risen up to take its rightful position, saying to his soul, "Now my soul, bless the Lord. Don't sit there in a sulk; don't sit there like a wet blanket, all melancholy and under the weather. Bless the Lord, and let everything that is within me bless His holy name."

I think of that marvelous little word in Luke 1:46 where you find that wonderful Magnificat of Mary: "My soul doth magnify the Lord, and my spirit hath rejoiced in God my Saviour."

Did you get that? Mary's worship of the Lord began in her spirit and spilled over into her soul.

Some people are frightened to death of the soul. Christians will say, "Oh, you must be very careful; it is soul." Now I must tell you that some places I go into, it is soul from beginning to end—gross, noisy soul. But then I go into other places where it is supposed to be all spirit. The soul has been so trampled upon that nobody is able to be normal. How can you be normal if your soul does not magnify the Lord? It is impossible. There is a certain branch of Christianity that would like to annihilate the soul, but you cannot deal with the spirit without the soul. Once the Holy Spirit, by the word of God, has done that surgery of dividing between spirit and soul, then what begins in the spirit can go over into the soul. And what do we get? We get hymns, and songs, and poetry, and ministry. We get all kinds of things. Where else do you think it comes from? You cannot do without the soul. It begins in the spirit, but it comes through the soul.

Spirit of Man

The word of God says, "The spirit of man is the candle of the Lord" (Proverbs 20:27). In other words, your spirit is the only essence in you and me that is of the same substance as God. It is why you and I are eternal, in one sense, undying; because when God breathed into man, He breathed something of His own being. I do not mean in a salvation way, but in our very creation we have a substance we call spirit, and this substance is the same substance as God.

> *He hath made everything beautiful in its time: also he hath set eternity in their heart, yet so that man cannot find out the work that God hath done from the beginning even to the end. Ecclesiastes 3:11*

Here you have a very difficult word, but in the Hebrew it is a little easier; it is *olam*. Some people say "the world," but that is nonsense. In Hebrew when we use this word *olam*, we mean "age abiding, something that goes beyond." God has put within man an empty vacuum, made of the same substance as Himself, and when it is indwelt by the Spirit of God, then a human being can begin to discover what the work of the Lord is all about. Until a man is born of God, his spirit is there but he cannot understand anything about it. That is why no human being can ever rest by being an animal. Even the most depraved human beings, who spend their whole time satisfying their physical appetites, have within them some kind of sense that they were meant for something more than this. It is "eternity" within their hearts; it is the spirit of the man. Even when debased, even when dead in trespasses and sins, even when alienated from God, yet that spirit of man is the vacuum that only God can fill. It does not matter what color a human being is, what nationality he is, what race he belongs to, if he fills that void with the world, with the things of life, with marriage, with home, with family, with career, with everything of time and sense, he is still unsatisfied.

That spirit within man was made for God. It can only ever be fulfilled when that man is born of God, when that spirit within him is raised to walk in newness of life, and the Spirit of the Lord comes in and dwells within him and brings about a union with God. How can I, a Jacob-like creature like me, flesh and blood, be joined to God who is Spirit? How is it possible for me to have a union with God who is eternal? How could it be possible for it to be said of me: "He that is joined to the Lord is one spirit"? How can spirit be joined to soul? How can the Spirit of the Lord be joined to flesh? When the spirit that God created me with is born of God and raised to walk in newness of life, it is joined to the Lord and becomes one spirit with the Lord. It is a most wonderful thing!

Even in fallen man, there are things within our spirit. There is a conscience in the spirit. The old Quakers used to say that there is a light within every unsaved man that is from God. They meant that the spirit of the man is the candle of the Lord. In that unsaved man is a conscience; and that conscience, even in the most unsaved man, will lead him to God, if he will only listen to it. But when there is a seared conscience or a hardened conscience, then the man loses all sensitivity, even to his conscience. When God created us, he placed a conscience in our spirit. This is what the unsaved men and women of the world who have never heard the gospel will be judged by in the day of the great judgment: how did they react to their conscience?

Also, in our spirit there is a thing called intuition. Sometimes it gets mixed up with the occult, with black magic, or Satanism. But intuition is something that God placed in our spirit. These three marvelous things—union with God, conscience, and intuition—are all in our spirit.

Soul of Man

We are not only spirit, we have a soul. Our souls, we could say, are our personalities, our temperaments. There are three things in our soul—emotion, will, and reasoning faculties. All of us live on one side or the other. Either we are very emotional and do not think things through too much, or we think things through very much and are not too emotional. Or we have wills like iron, which when wedded to emotion become horrifying, or when wedded to reasoning faculties can become just as horrifying. Yet God created us like this. He said, "But now thus saith the Lord that created thee, O Jacob." Jacob had a spirit, and in his spirit he had a conscience, but he did things against that conscience. He had an intuition, but he overrode it. Jacob still had all this capacity for union with God, yet he was not united with God. He had a soul, and in his soul he had emotion, he had will (Did he have will!), and he had reasoning power.

Body of Man

But God did not create you and me with merely a spirit and a soul. There are Christians who have this Greek idea which comes from Socrates and Aristotle and all the others and has gone right through the whole of western culture like a dose of salts. The attitude is that if you and I could only be done with the body, we would be pure. The spirit is pure; the flesh is wicked. And so you get many Christians with this diseased idea that anything to do with the body is evil, and everything to do with the spirit is pure. It is a strange thing that the Apostle Paul did not say, "I pray that God may preserve you wholly, that your entire spirit be saved in the day of Jesus Christ." Nor did he say, "I pray that your entire spirit and soul be saved in the day of Jesus Christ." But he said, "I pray that your entire spirit and soul and body be preserved entire in the day of Jesus Christ" (see 1 Thessalonians 5:23).

We have bodies. We are not going to be some kind of angelic creation one day. It is perfectly true we are going to have bodies. I cannot wait for it. We are going to have bodies that can go through walls, that can go up and go down, that can still eat things, and can recognize one another. Some people say, "Will we be able to recognize one another?" I think there will be a kind of inner intuition by which we shall know one another, even if we do not look quite the same. I know some people are dying for the day when they will not look quite the same! But we will still know one another. Anyway just suppose we didn't. Do you think our Lord would not introduce us? Within a few moments He would have angels going all the way through introducing so-and-so to so-and-so. But I do not think it will even be like that. I think we shall have something within us that will recognize one another. I will not need to be told who Abraham is; I will know him. And somehow I think I am going to know who Jeremiah is and who Isaiah is. I will not get Isaiah mixed up with Jeremiah, or Jeremiah mixed up with Isaiah.

When God created you with a body, it was to locate you. I know that is not always so, but still you are meant to be located. You are not meant to be wandering around in a kind of heavenly cloud, dreaming away. You are supposed to be located. Here you are; here is your body. You are sitting in a chair, and actually your spirit and your soul are located there. What a terrible business it would be if your spirit was wandering over there and your soul over here. If you want to get to me, you come to this body because that is where I am located. My body is the least thing about me, in one sense. It is my spirit and my soul that are the important parts of me. And one day I am going to be located in the new heaven and the new earth in the ages to come still in a redemption body. Think of that!

If you and I can only begin to understand something of God's original design in the creation of man, it will preserve us from a thousand errors. It will preserve us from the error of considering the things that are soulish are spiritual. It will preserve us from the error of thinking that we must destroy our soul in order to be spiritual. It will preserve us from the error of thinking that our bodies are unimportant. My dear friends, your body is tremendously important.

I cannot understand these Christians that get cremated. You will probably think I am being horribly superstitious, and then you will probably put it down to my being Jewish; but I think it is a terrible thing to be cremated. I do not mean by that you will not be raised. There are people who got burned in fires that could not help it. There are martyrs who were burned in fires in the inquisition and elsewhere, and God is going to raise them up, every part of their body. But I would never adopt a heathen custom. Such a custom has never been known amongst the people of God, because even Satan had an argument and a confrontation with the archangel Michael over the body of Moses. Most evangelical Christians would say, "What does it matter about Moses' body? He is in Paradise. He is with the Lord. Let Satan have his body. It is not worth anything anyway. The worms are going to eat it. It is going to go to dust." But that body of Moses was so precious that when Moses had gone into the presence of the Lord, Satan tried to obtain the body.

One day you will have a resurrection body. That is why it says in 1 Corinthians 15 that when we bury a body of a believer, we bury a miracle. It says, "We do not bury the body that shall be." But somehow, it is like a seed. That very body is going to be reconstituted in a miracle of resurrection power and glory one day—a body without sin, a body that is a resurrection body and yet still a human body. Our lovely Lord Jesus has as human a body as ever He had. He even has the marks still in His hands and in His side and in His feet. It is not a different body. It is the body that He walked with here on this earth, but it is a resurrection body.

How marvelous it is just to consider for a few moments the original design of God when He said to Jacob, "But now thus saith the Lord that created thee, O Jacob." You may have fallen, sin may have gotten into you, you may be alive to the powers of darkness, demonic forces may be influencing you, but still, God created you spirit, soul and body, and there is a way out for you.

Tree of Life

Do you remember that there was a tree of life in the garden of Eden? I, myself, have no doubt there was an actual tree. I do not have any problems with this since it was an actual garden, and an actual allotment of earth with actual plants in it, and they were actually tending it. It seems to me that there was an actual tree. But I do not think it was an apple tree. Some people say in my part of the world that it was an orange tree. We are not told, but God took a tree and He made that tree symbolic of something. It was not that the tree itself was something, but He took it and said, "If you eat of that tree, you will live forever." It is symbolic of something. Near it was another tree—the tree of the knowledge of good and evil. God said of that tree, "If you eat of that tree, you shall surely die." God's original plan for man was that in some marvelous way, he should be led by the Spirit of God to partake of the tree of life. Or to put it in terms we would all understand, he would come to receive the Lord Jesus. He would become one who would be born of the Spirit of God.

When Adam was created, he was created innocent, and he was created sinless; but he was not created perfect. In other words, he was created without sin, and he was created innocent; but if he wanted to be a complete human being, he had to take certain steps by faith. There was a positive, and there was a negative.

There was the tree of life. God never said to him, You shall not eat of the tree of life. There was the tree of the knowledge of good and evil. God said, "You shall not eat of the tree of the knowledge of good and evil, for in the day you eat thereof you shall surely die."

What did God mean, "You shall surely die"? Adam did not die in the day that he ate of the tree of the knowledge of good and evil. Actually, Adam lived to nearly a thousand years of age. Does that make God a liar? What God meant was that in the day that Adam chose to be a self-centered, self-dependent, self-conscious man, he died spiritually. The tree of life is symbolic of another kind of man—God-centered, God-dependent, God-conscious. Let me put it another way that you will understand better— Christ-centered, Christ-dependent, Christ-conscious. That was the kind of man God intended Adam to be.

Fallen Man

Trees in the Bible are always symbolic of men. The tree of life was symbolic of one kind of Man, and the tree of the knowledge of good and evil was symbolic of another kind of man. And in the garden of Eden, Adam and Eve made a choice. What happened? In that day when man fell, his spirit died but it was not annihilated. Some people think that when a man's spirit is dead because of sin, it is no longer there. That is nonsense! What it means is this. If I took one of these electric light bulbs out of its socket and put it here on this little rostrum and said to you, "Is there an electric light bulb there?"

You would say, "Yes."

I would say, "Is it the same as those electric light bulbs up there?"

And you would say, "As far as we know, yes."

"Then why doesn't it give light? If it is still an electric light bulb, how come it does not give light and those do?"

You say, "Because it is not screwed in the socket."

It is as simple as that. The bulb is still a bulb, but it is divorced or alienated from the current. When Adam and Eve fell, they were alienated from God. They were divorced from eternal life. They were divorced from the Person and life of God. It does not mean they no longer had a spirit; but it means that their spirit was not functioning.

The Bible is very, very clear on this whole thing: "Flesh and blood cannot inherit the kingdom of God; neither doth corruption inherit incorruption" (1 Corinthians 15:50). This is not just flesh and blood but the whole fallen man, this kind of man that we have become. If you think about it for a moment you will understand the whole of human history. It is not a question of whether you are good or bad, it is a question of what kind of man you are. The best, even the most noble, have a fallen nature. We are self-centered, self-dependent, self-conscious.

Do you remember the first thing that Adam and Eve did when they fell? They sewed leaves. What a ridiculous thing to do! They went out, took leaves from the trees, sewed them together, and made shorts. The old version says britches, but it means shorts. They were self-conscious. They had never been self-conscious before. That was the first thing that happened.

The second thing: they did it themselves. They never went to the Lord and said, "Lord, what shall we do? We have done a terrible thing." They talked it over and produced something themselves.

The most interesting thing of all was that Adam said, "It was not me, Lord; it was her." And she said, "It was not me, Lord; it was the serpent that you put in the garden." Self-centeredness. I have no doubt that Adam loved Eve, but the moment it came to his life it was self first. "If there is anyone who is going to be judged, it should be her, Lord. I would never have done it but for her. You know these women. They are so clever, so cunning, and so full of guile. Well, You created her, Lord."

What had happened to Adam? He had become a self-centered man. And Eve more or less said, "Lord, it is Your fault. Who put the serpent in the garden in the first place?"

Do you remember what the Lord said to them? "In the day that you eat thereof you shall surely die" (see Genesis 2:17). Do you remember what the serpent said to Eve? "Has the Lord said, 'In the day that you eat thereof you shall surely die'? You shall not die, but you shall be as God, knowing good and evil" (see Genesis 3). What Satan said was a half-truth. He said, "If you choose to be the kind of man that is represented by this tree of the knowledge of good and evil, you will have the center inside of yourselves. You will not need God. You will be like little gods." This is the whole of human history. All the way down through the thousands of years of man's history it has been this kind of man that has been seen, even in his noblest expression and in his most depraved and evil expression.

The Last Adam

Thank God there is another kind of Man because the Bible says that Jesus is the last Adam! He is called the last Adam and the second Man, as if there is no other man. It is as if God is saying, "As far as I am concerned, the first man and everyone that came out of him is put away. Now we have a new beginning, a second Man, and out of Him will come many sons being brought to glory through His own work, and with His own nature and life in them." When you begin to see it like that, I suggest to you that the New Testament begins to take on a quite different meaning.

For instance, in 1 Corinthians 15:45–49 it says, "So also it is written, the first man Adam became a living soul. The last Adam became a life-giving spirit. Howbeit that is not first which is spiritual, but that which is natural; then that which is spiritual. The first man is of the earth, earthy: the second man is of heaven. As is the earthy, such are they also that are earthy: and as is the heavenly, such are they also that are heavenly. And as we have borne the image of the earthy, we shall also bear the image of the heavenly."

> *For since by man came death, by man came also the resurrection of the dead. For as in Adam all die, so also in Christ shall all be made alive. 1 Corinthians 15:21–22*

No wonder God could say to Jacob, "But now thus saith the Lord that created thee, O Jacob, and he that formed thee, O Israel: Fear not, for I have redeemed thee; I have called thee by thy name, thou art mine."

We are living in a day in which we are going to see this kind of man, symbolized by the tree of the knowledge of good and evil, brought to complete and full fruition. If the Lord does not rapture us before, we are going to see the most horrifying things done by man to man in the name of progress. Already we see it in abortion. It is because God has created every human being in His image that He has a claim on them, even though fallen and depraved.

All human beings have to answer to the Creator over what they have done with their bodies, whether they have abused their bodies with sex, or drugs, or by abortion, or other perversions. Every human being is answerable to God because God says, "I created you." Marx created no man, nor did Mao Tse-tung, nor did the Ayatollah Khomeini, nor have any of the others. God has the supreme claim of every human being, whether they believe in Him or not, because He has created them.

We are moving into days when we will see this man, symbolized by the tree of the knowledge of good and evil, overcoming all kinds of things. It is horrifying what genetically now can be done. It is not actually being thus far divulged to the general public because it is so horrifying. I suppose you know that within six years they believe a man will be able to give birth to a baby. They are going to change the whole fabric of life, just as it says in the word: "They will change the seasons."

God dealt a death blow, in one sense, to this fallen man thousands of years ago in a great civilization called Babel when they built a tower. We do not know what they were doing with that tower, whether it was astrological, astronomical, or man's first attempt to get into space. But whatever it was, we know that they were trying to join earth and heaven. And God said, "If we let them do this thing, nothing will be withheld from them." So He blasted the whole thing, and they all spoke different languages. This has amazingly arrested fallen man over thousands of years, but today we are overcoming it. The degeneration of man physically is being overcome by medical science. We are exploring space. We are overcoming the problem of languages. We can, through the medium of television bounced off satellites, bring the whole world to watch events and prepare them for some kind of world government in the end, and through the media, create a world public opinion.

I am glad I belong to another Man. I am glad I belong to the new Man. I am glad I have been born by the grace of God into the kingdom of God. Aren't you? We are His by creation. That is the first claim He has on you and me. Therefore, let us never despise what He has created. We have a spirit. May God bring our spirits into such a union with Him that we shall know His indwelling so powerfully that we shall be enabled to take our place over our souls and bodies. We will be able to say to our souls, "Be still." We will be able to say to our souls, "I am going to wean you." It is going to be a job, just like the weaning of any child is a job. "You, my soul, are going to become the vehicle for everything that God does in my spirit." It is sad when a kind of inhibition comes among God's people. There are no songs written, no poems, no communication, and no creativity; as if being spiritual is to be a kind of static state in which we do nothing. But when we look into the history of the church, every time the Holy Spirit has taken over, every time the Lord Jesus has been re-enthroned, there has been an outburst of new hymns, new songs, new worship, new praise, and new creativity.

What is a spiritual man? A spiritual man is a man whose spirit, in union with the Spirit of God, in union with the Lord Jesus, is governing his soul and his body. Brothers and sisters, let us take care of this earthen vessel. An earthen vessel it may be, but it is a temple of the living God. Let us not devalue it nor despise it, but let us make it to be a manifestation of the beauty of the Lord our God. "But now thus saith the Lord that created thee, O Jacob ... thou art mine."

Let us pray:

Heavenly Lord, we thank You for helping us to overcome some of the more unusual circumstances, and we pray that You will write in our hearts something of Your word. For some of us, Lord, there is nothing new about what has been said. But use what has been said to elucidate and clear up and clarify and define things for us. For others of us, Lord, it may have come to us as something quite new. Bring it to us with all the force of revelation. Preserve us from misinterpretation or any kind of extreme kind of interpretation. Lord, will You, in Your own wonderful way, bring us face to face with the fact that You have created each one of us, and You have created us for your glory—spirit, soul, and body? Do this wonderful work in revealing these things to us; and not only revealing it to us but, Lord, making it flesh and blood within us. We ask it in the name of our Lord, Jesus Christ. Amen.

2.
Thou Art Mine By Redemption

Isaiah 43:1–2

But now thus saith the Lord that created thee, O Jacob, and he that formed thee, O Israel: Fear not, for I have redeemed thee; I have called thee by thy name, thou art mine. When thou passest through the waters, I will be with thee; and through the rivers, they shall not overflow thee: when thou walkest through the fire, thou shalt not be burned, neither shall the flame kindle upon thee.

Shall we bow in a word of prayer:

Heavenly Father, we are so glad that when it comes to the speaking of Your word and the hearing of Your word, You have not left us to our own energies, or to our own talents or gifts. But You have provided us, speaker and hearer, with an anointing, and we want to come very simply to avail ourselves of that anointing. We thank You, Lord, that Your divine grace and power can so tabernacle upon us that Your purpose can be fulfilled, and Your intention and design in our time realized. That is what we ask, Lord—not for just some routine meeting, but a meeting with Yourself. We pray that Your Holy Spirit will, Himself, tabernacle upon our physical weakness and cause the beauty and grace of our Lord Jesus to be communicated to us. We ask it in His precious name. Amen.

The little phrase that has burned its way into my heart is contained in this first verse of Isaiah 43: "Thou art mine." There are four ways in which the Lord claims us as His own. We are His by creation, we are His by redemption, we are His by calling, and we are His through overcoming. These are the four ways that the Lord is showing something of this matter to me, and I am seeking, by His grace, to share and communicate to you.

We are going to consider the second way the Lord claims us as His. "But now thus saith the Lord that created thee, O Jacob, and he that formed thee, O Israel: Fear not, for I have redeemed thee." Only God could form an Israel out of Jacob. Moses could not do it, none of the prophets could do it, not even the apostles could ever form an Israel out of Jacob. Nobody could form a prince with God—not only by pedigree, not only by blood, but by essential, inward character. Nobody but God could take a Jacob and form him into an Israel. That is exactly what God has done with you and me. Some of us may not yet recognize that we are Jacobs. We might consider ourselves a cut above Jacob, but if we go on with the Lord, we shall have to come to the conclusion that we are Jacobs by nature. And the marvelous thing is that God takes Jacobs and forms Israels out of them, something only God could ever conceive of doing.

There is only one explanation for this determination of God to form Israel out of Jacob. If I were the Lord, I would have finished with Jacob. I would have started all over again with better material. Why bother with twisted, deceiving, supplanting material? Why not just be done with it and start all over again with something nice and pure, something nice and clean, something with no twistedness in it? If I were the Lord, I would never put up with the murmuring of God's people. I would boot them out. I would give them one or two warnings and then boot the lot out. But that is because I do not have the grace that God has. It is an amazing thing to come to this one conclusion only. It is abounding, fathomless, amazing, unmerited, undeserved grace. Only grace of that kind could take a person like Jacob and form an Israel out of him. Think of the patience required. Think of the wisdom required. Think of the power required. Think of the determination required. Yet it is the Lord that says, "But now thus saith the Lord that created thee, O Jacob, and he that formed thee, O Israel: Fear not, for I have redeemed thee." It is the redeeming grace and power of God that settles its love upon a Jacob and forms an Israel out of the most unlikely material. If God had wanted to, when Adam fell, He could have blown the whole creation to smithereens with one great divine nuclear explosion, and then by another word, started all over again. But God is not like that. The glory of God is that He perseveres; He is determined. We can only call this the determination of divine love. There is no other explanation for it.

I have long since given up trying philosophically or even theologically to understand the words: "Jacob have I loved, but Esau have I hated." I can only understand this extraordinary thing about love. I have never been able to understand what some people love in somebody else. I see the most extraordinary things as I go around the world. I see men in love with women that are cross-eyed, shapeless; and yet, they are absolutely in love with them. I see women in love with men that really makes me wonder, "What do they see in the man?" But love is the most extraordinary thing.

It is not in the Bible, but we know so well the words, "Beauty is in the eye of the beholder." And in one sense, we have to say that about God. I do not know why He loves you or why He loves me. As I have gone on with the Lord, I have come to the conclusion that it is amazing that He loves me. I do not know what He sees. Why didn't He finish with us and start all over again with someone not quite so twisted, someone not quite so rebellious, someone not quite so devious, someone not quite so difficult?

Sometimes it takes the Lord a lifetime to get some of us to our Jabbok. Supposing the Lord could get us at the beginning of our teens, change us, and have a whole life in front of us. But no, we are such devious, difficult people. We fight with the Lord, we wrestle with the Lord, we avoid the Lord, and we refuse to face the issues. Sometimes it is a lifetime before the Lord finally gets us on the deathbed, and yet, apparently, it is all worth it to the Lord if He finally gets us.

Conformed to the Image of God's Son

The forming of Israel out of Jacob is an amazing thing. If I could think of Jacob as something on one side and Israel as something altogether different, it would make it a little easier. But in actual fact, Israel is only Jacob with another name, and yet, it is more than another name. Something has happened to Jacob. He is still Jacob, and God is still pleased to call Himself the God of Jacob. He still says, "I love Jacob"; but Israel is Jacob. Only the grace of God has transformed him. To put it in New Testament terms: he is being conformed to the image of God's Son.

You can go to a thousand seminaries, go through a thousand theological courses, you can attend a thousand different denominational meetings, and then leave them for interdenominational meetings, and then leave them for non-denominational meetings; but it is all without any worth unless you are being conformed to the image of God's Son. You can discuss theology until you are blue in the face, you can split the finer points of the word of God, you can preach, you can exercise faith, you can understand mysteries, but if you are not being changed, it is worthless. In the end, it is not the position you have down here, or the status you occupy, the status that is given to you, but it is whether the Lord is forming Israel out of Jacob.

One day when this little life is all over and gone, you will look back and you will see that the only thing that was worthwhile in this life was the work God did in you and me in conforming us to the image of His Son because that is forever. Everything else falls away. Everything—the job that worries you, the career you are fighting for, the reputation you are seeking to uphold, even the marriage that you have—will dissolve with death. Nothing goes through into eternity but what God does in your life and in my life. And Jacob, though created spirit, soul and body, though originally created in the image of God, cannot inherit the kingdom of God in himself. Only Israel can inherit the kingdom of God. It is only when God has conformed you to the image of His Son that you can inherit the kingdom of God. It is only what God, by His Spirit, has done in you and in me that goes through into eternity.

Sinners into Saints

It is the work of God to turn sinners into saints. Now I do not mean those pale, emaciated, effeminate-looking creatures that stare down at us from stained glass windows. When I was a child, the only idea I ever had of Christianity was of that. I thought all Christians were pale, emaciated, and spineless. Of course, it is true that there are an awful lot of God's people who are pale and colorless. They have a kind of religious spirit, a kind of artificial Christianity that altogether inhibits them from becoming the people that God wants them to be. That is why the Lord's people are so uninteresting sometimes and why the world can be so interesting. In the world, even in its fallen state, there are real people. They are wicked, cunning, and devious, but they are real. When you come into some of these Christian assemblies, you do not meet real people. You only meet shadows, shells, projected images, or what they consider as spiritual. No, I am not talking about that kind of saint.

The saints that God is making out of sinners are real people, such as Matthew who was a tax collector. I have never yet met a tax collector who is not a bit of a character, and Jewish tax collectors are undoubtedly the best in the world.

Or I think of Peter, the fisherman. In my travels, I have always found two types of men that are quite interesting: fishermen and shepherds. When I have gone to New Zealand, I have never yet met a shepherd who was not an interesting character, and it is the same with fishermen. Maybe it is being close to the elements. But Peter was a character, and he remained one to the end. Do you remember when he had that bust-up with Paul, publicly, over whether to be kosher or not to be kosher? At the very end, when he wrote the letter, he said, "Our beloved brother, Paul, who writes things very hard to understand." So many Christians would not dream of saying anything like that. We iron that kind of thing out.

Or I think of Paul. He was an incredible character. The man was a saint, not only by position, but also in character. Peter had become a saint, not just in position, but in character. Israel was formed out of Jacob in them.

Paul is such a real person. He writes in one of his letters: "You are pushing me to boast." How many Christians would ever write a letter like that, especially if they have read a few books by Mr. Sparks? They would not dream of saying, "You are pushing me to boast." But Paul writes his letter to the Corinthians and says, "You are just getting me into such a position that I have to boast. I do not come one whit behind any of these other big people you call apostles." Then he goes through the whole catalog. I imagine Paul having a bad time after he had posted the letter. Of course, He did not realize that it was Scripture. I can just imagine him rolling in bed and thinking, "Oh, how could I do that? What a dreadful thing I have said in letting the cat out of the bag like that. I should never have done it. I have exposed myself before all those saints." And supposing some angel had said to him, "Paul, all down through the centuries saints are going to study what you have written." This is not a stained-glass saint. This is a real saint. The man was a sinner turned into a saint. It is an Israel formed out of a Jacob.

That is why I say, even if our meetings down here are fearfully boring at times, heaven above will never be boring. Just imagine it: Jacob is there along with Moses and David. And I think of that extraordinary lady I wish to meet, Jael, the one who drove a peg through that man's head. Some Christians are going to get such a shock when they get up there. I think of some of the real saints I have known in my little life—not these stained-glass people. I dare say, if we had a testimony meeting in heaven lasting a thousand years, not one of us would go to sleep.

God is not interested in the artificial, the unreal, the pseudo, the facade. He is interested in Jacobs. "What is thy name?" said the angel of the Lord when he wrestled with Jacob. Now isn't that silly, as if the angel of the Lord did not know whom he was wrestling with? The Lord had said to him, "Now get down there; he is going to come to Jabbok. You get a grip on him and do not let him go. You know who it is, don't you? It is not Esau; it is Jacob you are going to get hold of." Then the angel said, "What is thy name?" Of course, the whole point was not for the angel's sake. He knew exactly whom he was wrestling with. It was to find out whether Jacob had finally come down to the basis of total reality. Jacob could have said, "I am Abraham's grandson." That would have gotten him some credit. Or maybe he could have said, "I am Isaac's son." But he said: "My name is Jacob." Then the Lord said, "That is enough; you will no more be Jacob; you shall be Israel."

It is the glory of God to turn sinners into saints. The process is costly, but it is the glory of God to turn sinners into saints.

For whom He foreknew, he also foreordained to be conformed to the image of his Son, that he might be the firstborn among many brethren: and whom he foreordained, them he also called: and whom he called, them he also justified: and whom he justified, them he also glorified. Romans 8:29–30

So all the predestinating grace and power of God is behind the transformation of Jacob into Israel. "But now thus saith the Lord that created thee, O Jacob, and he that formed thee, O Israel: Fear not, for I have redeemed thee."

Jacob the Twister

The name Jacob in Hebrew, *Yaaqob*, means "twister." That is how I put it in colloquial English. Actually in the King James English it really means "supplanter." Jacob was born with his arm twisted around his brother's leg, seeking somehow or other to pull his brother back so that he could be first. He did not quite manage it, and they called him *Yaaqob*—"twister, supplanter."

It was the grace of God that took Jacob, the supplanter, and turned him into the builder because, in the Jewish tradition, Jacob is called the builder of the house of Israel. Now there is such a difference between a destroyer, a supplanter, and a builder. Can you think of anything more disparate than a supplanter, or a destroyer, and a builder?

For instance, Jacob destroyed his brother's birthright; he stole it. Of course, Esau sold it "for a mess of pottage" as it is put in the King James Version. That is how much he thought of it; that is how much he valued it. Nevertheless, Jacob destroyed his brother's right.

Later, he stole his brother's blessing. What a story! Mother was in on the act, stitching things up all night. The bit of goat's skin she chose had to be very special. She must have gone looking all around the flocks to find a special texture. Then she spent the whole time sewing it exactly so it would go on like a glove over Jacob's arms. Poor old blind Isaac would feel the arms of Jacob and think it was Esau. Rebekah and Jacob were both in on the act, planning the whole thing together. It ran in the family.

You do not call a destroyer a builder of the house of Israel. You do not ever build the house of God by stealing the birthrights of others, supplanting others. The house of God is not a place for ambition, a place where we push others down in order to come up. That is not the house of God. And yet, this Jacob became the builder of the house of Israel. Forever afterwards, God's chosen people are called by his new name, Israel.

Jacob the Blesser

I think of Jacob, the twister, the twisted; and this Jacob becomes the blesser and the worshipper.

> *By faith Jacob, when he was dying, blessed each*
> *of the sons of Joseph; and worshipped, leaning*
> *upon the top of his staff. Hebrews 11:21*

The Hebrew actually says "leaning on his bedpost"; but whether it was his staff or his bedpost, it does not really matter. Jacob had been touched in his thigh, and his thigh was put out of joint for the rest of his life. He limped for the rest of his days. But the twister had become a blesser, and the twister had become a worshiper.

Is there anything more disparate, more different, than a person who is a twister, and someone who blesses other people? Have you ever met anybody who is a twister that has been a blessing? I have not. They normally take things from you rather than giving things to you. This was very true of Jacob. He lifted (stole) his brother's birthright, he lifted his brother's blessing, and he lifted his uncle's sheep and goats. That was his nature—acquisitive. He was always acquiring. He could not help it; it was his nature. He did not sit down and think out the methods by which he acquired things. He had such a feeling of desire and covetousness to get things that as long as he got them that was all that mattered. But at the end of his life this Jacob became a blesser; and when he blessed those two sons of Joseph, it was a real blessing. Something came upon them that never left them. I think one of the most beautiful chapters in the whole of the Old Testament is Genesis 49 when Jacob blessed his twelve sons, one by one. Oh, he had such a prophetic revelation, such a word of knowledge, such a word of wisdom, such an insight into the future and destiny of each of those men and of the tribes that would come out of them. The old twister had become a blesser. Only God could form a blesser out of a twister.

Jacob the Worshiper

It also says of Jacob that he worshiped. Have you ever noticed that when there is a lot of twistedness in us, we cannot worship? Worship, by its very nature, takes us out of ourselves, and we give. Just as we give in blessing to one another, so when we worship, we give to God. When we are twisted and a twister, we cannot do it. But something has happened to the twister; he has become a worshiper.

I always thought it very amazing when Jacob was first sent away from his family and fled for his life from his twin brother, Esau, that he lay down in a place just north of Jerusalem. He took one of the stones for a pillow, and to this day there are so many stones there you would have no problem in selecting one. He put his head on it, and he went into a weary, restless sleep. He saw the Lord, and he said, "This is none other than the house of God." But he was afraid. He built an altar, and he called the place *Bethel*, "house of God." He said, "Lord, if You will only keep me in this journey I will come back here and build You a house." He could not help it. It was tit for tat. He wanted something: "You look after me, Lord, and I will look after You. You keep me in the country I am going to, and I will build You a house." But at the end of his life, he was a worshiper.

This whole matter of Israel being formed out of Jacob means something to me because I think, "If He can do it with Jacob, He can do it with me."

"Fear not, for I have redeemed thee." Why does the Lord say, "Fear not"? Is that an intimation that there are times when Jacob wonders: "Can the redeeming grace of God and love of God persevere with me? Am I perhaps too twisted for God, too complex for the Lord? Maybe my genetic history is too much of a problem for the Lord, or the kind of personality and type of temperament I have. Maybe the family life I have had, my mother is too much for the Lord." Rebekah was some lady. Of course, you see it in her brother, Laban. They were all part of the same family—quite remarkable people. I wonder whether you have a little intimation in that word: "Fear not, for I have redeemed thee." Perhaps there were times when Jacob would be tempted to say, "I am too much for the Lord; better for Him to find a Moses or someone like my father, Isaac, or someone like Enoch."

The Redeemer

"Fear not, Jacob, I have redeemed thee." This word, redemption, is a word that somehow has gotten devalued amongst us. I do not think we always realize what a wonderful word redemption is. Salvation has within it the idea of being made whole; but redemption has within it the idea of being retrieved, recovered, liberated.

When the children of Israel went into Egypt, they became slaves to Pharaoh; they became his bond-slaves. And God redeemed them with an outstretched arm, by His power. They were the Lord's, but somehow or other they had come into a place they should never have been. They were God's servants; they were God's sons; but they had become bond-slaves of the powers of darkness. They had become involved in this world.

They had become part and parcel of the fabric and the system of this world.

And then God said: "I will redeem them and bring them up out of Egypt. I will send My servant, Moses, to Pharaoh and say, 'Let My people go.'"

In this word, redemption, there is this glorious thought of retrieving, recovering, liberating, freeing, delivering. If you were a slave in the market, you could be redeemed if someone would only pay the price. You and I are all slaves in the market of this world. We are, by nature, Jacobs, though marked out by the love of God, and chosen before the foundation of the world. Still, we are lost in sin, dead in trespasses and sins; and then comes the Redeemer. Moses could never have been the redeemer, nor could any of the prophets. The only one who could redeem us was Jesus. "Fear not," the Lord says to you and to me, "I have redeemed thee; thou art mine."

Do you know the price that the Lord paid for you was total? And do you know the Lord would have paid that price if you had been the only one? That is the whole point in telling the story of the man who had a hundred sheep: ninety-nine were safe and one was out. The Lord has redeemed you; do not fear. If God has given so much to retrieve you, to recover you, to liberate you, don't you think that He is going to put at your disposal every single bit of grace and power you need to be conformed to the image of God's Son?

Justification

In the New Testament we find some very interesting things concerning this matter of redemption.

For all have sinned, and fall short of the glory of God; being justified freely by his grace through the redemption that is in Christ Jesus. Romans 3:23–24

In whom we have our redemption through his blood, the forgiveness of our trespasses according to the riches of his grace. Ephesians 1:7

Who delivered us out of the power of darkness, and translated us into the kingdom of the Son of his love; in whom we have our redemption, the forgiveness of our sins. Colossians 1:13–14

I do not know why, but the work of the cross, in its fulness, is often looked upon as kindergarten amongst believers. The tragedy is that in today's Christianity there is very little understanding of justification. We imagine that it has something to do with the kindergarten, and we think, "Well, we know all about that. We want the deeper things."

But God can never start to form Israel out of Jacob unless He has a very solid foundation upon which Jacob can stand while the work is being done. It is all very well to talk about being crucified with Christ. It is all very well to talk about laying down one's life for Him and for the gospel. It is all very well to talk about falling into the ground and dying. It is all very well to talk about being broken through the work of the cross; but woe betide anyone who begins to experience the subjective work of the cross if he does not know the objective work of the cross.

Let me put it another way. If you do not know what it is to be justified through the death of the Lord Jesus on the cross, then once the Holy Spirit starts to apply the work of the cross subjectively in the way you have got to learn to die, you will come to the place where you will break up. No man or woman can ever see themselves as God sees them unless they know that they are justified. God dare not take aside the veil and show us what we are. We would go into a mental home within days. We are all so self-righteous. We have no idea how self-righteous we are. We do not recognize what we are capable of. We only think so-and-so is capable of that; so-and-so is capable of that. We would never think we could be capable of doing such a thing if subjected to the same pressures. But God knows the depths that are within us.

He could never show Jacob what he was like until he reached a certain place in his life. Jacob was scandalized by his Uncle Laban. He could not believe it. "I have worked for him," he said, "for years, slaved my hands to the bone that I might marry his younger daughter. And then, that big-time twister dressed up Leah to look like Rachel and married off his older daughter to me." If it were not in the Bible, you would not believe it. People with a Western tradition always come and say: "I do not understand it. How did Jacob not spot that it was Leah?" First of all, they did not have electricity in those days. Secondly, they did not belong to temperance societies. I am not saying that Jacob was drunk;

I am just saying that the wedding rites used to go on for a whole week.

It was the biggest shock poor old Jacob ever got when he woke up in the morning and there was Leah and not Rachel. He was scandalized: "How could my own flesh and blood, my uncle, my mother's brother, do something like that? If he were just an employer I would understand it; but my own flesh and blood, my uncle? He twisted me over the matters of the heart. To twist me for money I can understand; to twist me out of property I can understand; and even to twist me out of those goats and sheep; but to twist me out of the one person I desired to be joined to and to live with—it is scandalous."

Apparently, Jacob never thought of what he had done: "It was my twin brother—not even my brother, but my twin brother that I stole the birthright from. It was my twin brother and my godly old half-blind father that I deceived." It never entered his head.

In the Lord's work, I have often been surprised how blind the people I work with are to themselves. Of course, they think I am blind to myself. But isn't it amazing just how blind we sometimes are to what is glaringly obvious to everybody who knows us?

Why do you think the Lord did not tear aside the whole veil right at the beginning and say, "Jacob, come and stand here; I am going to draw aside the veil and show you as you really are." Poor old Jacob would have gone clean out of his head. He would have reeled under the impact of seeing what he really was like in such a way that it would have blown his whole mental health and balance.

God is often hampered with you and me. He cannot really begin to show us what we are like in such a way that we say, "Lord, I will not let You go until you do something. I have no other answer but to go on with You. I cannot go back, Lord. Now, that I have seen what I am like, there is no going back. I have got to go on; and if You do not do something to me, then I am finished."

The Lord is often hampered from showing us what we are like because we do not understand justification. We are so self-righteous that if we really saw what we were capable of, it would be the biggest shock we have ever had. We would never be able to pray again, never be able to sing another hymn again, never be able to fellowship again. We would say, "I cannot do it, I cannot do it. Now I know what I am like." And we would have a strange idea that it has come as a great shock to the Lord. "Do not tell Him, because He thinks I am a sweet little thing. I kneel beside my bed and say my prayers. I try to do my best." Actually, the Lord knows the worst in you, and He loves you. "But now thus saith the Lord that created thee, O Jacob, and he that formed thee, O Israel: Fear not, for I have redeemed thee."

Covering

The atoning death of our Lord Jesus is the most wonderful thing in the whole Bible. In Hebrew, the word *atonement* just means "covering." Yom Kippur is the day of atonement, day of covering. In that one death for all, Jesus covered all our sins. He took it all into Himself and bore it away. God has declared that you and I are justified. You know the old thing they used to say, at least when I was first saved, "Justified, just as if you had never sinned."

Listen to these wonderful words in II Corinthians 5:21: "Him who knew no sin he made to be sin on our behalf; that we might become the righteousness of God in him."

He made the One who knew no sin to be our sin that you and I might become the righteousness of God, God's righteousness in Him. It is a transfer. God took your sin and put it on the Lord Jesus and took the righteousness of the Lord Jesus and put it on you; and when you are in Christ, you are covered. You have the garment of salvation upon you. You are actually covered so that God only sees the righteousness and holiness of the Lord Jesus. When God looked at the Lord Jesus, He saw your sins and He smote Him, according to the word: "I will strike the shepherd." What a glorious thing it is then when the Lord says to you and me: "Fear not for I have redeemed thee. I have paid the price. I have become your sin and paid the price of your sin, and My righteousness is now yours."

The Scripture says some marvelous things about this:

I have blotted out, as a thick cloud, thy transgressions,
and, as a cloud, thy sins: return unto me; for
I have redeemed thee. Isaiah 44:22

I, even I, am he that blotteth out thy transgressions for mine
own sake; and I will not remember thy sins. Isaiah 43:25

They are blotted out and remembered no more. It is as if you came to the Lord and said, "Do you remember, Lord, when I did so-and-so and so-and-so, and when I sinned?" And the Lord will say to you, "I do not know what you are talking about." Atoned, covered.

> It says in another place: "Come now and let us reason together, saith the Lord: though your sins be as scarlet, they shall be as white as snow. Isaiah 1:18

It is only because the Lord has done this great work that He can form an Israel out of a Jacob. He dare not start the work of transformation unless you understand His redemption. He dare not start the work of uncovering what you are so that you see there is no going back, there is no other alternative, and the Lord is your only hope, unless you understand His redemption.

Crucified with Christ

There is another thing to His redemption. I am not at all sure that the New Testament has so neatly divided the subjective work of the cross from the objective work of the cross as some of us would like to think.

I think of these wonderful words in Galatians 2:20: "I have been crucified with Christ; and it is no longer I that live, but Christ liveth in me: and that life which I now live in the flesh I live in faith, the faith which is in the Son of God, who loved me, and gave himself up for me."

There are two things here—"I have been crucified with Christ" and "the Son of God, who loved me, and gave himself for me."

I do not know about you, but I will tell you what I think is the problem in my life. It is not just sin; it is "I." Have you come to that conclusion yet? The problem is me—I: I want, I will, I will not, I shall, I think, it is my opinion.

How can Jacob, the most "I" person in the Old Testament, ever become Israel, a prince with God, reigning with God? How can he become Israel unless God deals with the "I"? And God did; He wrestled with him and put his thigh out of joint.

Of course, sometimes we get the idea that God just wants to destroy the "I" altogether. When I was first saved, they used to sing a hymn that I, in my frame of mind, with my kind of background, used to find terribly funny. I would see all these grownups singing their hearts out, "Channels Only, blessed Master, channels only." I would imagine some kind of little drainpipe, and I used to think, "What an extraordinary thing, all these people singing, *Channels Only*." And it got so far into many of them that they decided they must not be personalities at all. They were really quite colorless, a lot of them. They could hardly say "boo" to a goose. They had really become channels only. The trouble was that the Lord did not come through. Now if the Lord had come through, and the channels had been flooded over with the Lord, that would have been something. But apparently, their idea of being a Christian was to be a little kind of drainpipe, nothing more than a channel.

I think the Lord would have a very easy time if He could only reduce us to being channels, if that were His plan and design. Just pulverize us until we are nothing, until we are little channels or little pipes. But the Lord did not create us like that. He created us with emotions, and with will and with reasoning powers. It is not quite so easy. Furthermore, when He has done the work in our spirit, He wants to reclaim our emotions, our will power, and even our reasoning powers so they all come under the government of the Holy Spirit. That is not so easy as being a channel only. I understand what the hymn writer meant, now that I have gotten a little older in the Lord.

Some people get the idea that I have been crucified and it is not I anymore; I am gone. Unfortunately, it is not as easy as that. It would be so lovely if we had some kind of spiritual wand that we could wave over congregations and say, "No more I." But it does not work like that.

"I have been crucified with Christ; nevertheless, I live. Yet not I." Oh dear, I do wish Paul would be clearer. Sometimes I feel that he gets us into such a mess. "I have been crucified with Christ; nevertheless, I live. Yet not I, but Christ liveth in me." Now what do you mean, Paul? Is it I or not I? Really, what Paul is saying is this: The "I," the big "I" with the I-life has been crucified with Christ; and the broken "I" still lives in Christ. There is still an "I" that lives in Christ. That is why John could say, "I, John;" and Paul could say in another place in one of his letters, "I, Paul." This work of the cross is absolutely essential if God is going to form Israel out of Jacob. If God is going to conform me to the image of His Son, His biggest problem is me. I must come to the place where I will say to the Lord, "OK Lord, when You died, I died; do Your work."

Sometimes young Christians come to me and say: "Oh, I have such a problem about living the Christian life. I do not know how to live it; that is my problem. Can you tell me how to live the Christian life?" And I always say to them, "Your problem is not how to live; your problem is how to die." If you can learn the secret of how to die daily, the living will take care of itself. The law of the cross is this: if you go down, you will come up; if you humble yourself, God will exalt you; if you lose your reputation, God will preserve your reputation in the end; if you become a doormat, you will, in the end, sit on the throne; if you go down into the depths, God will raise you to the heights; if you want to be whole, you must know what it is to be broken; if you want to know power, you must know what it is to be weak. That is the law, the unchanging law of the cross.

> *But we have this treasure in earthen vessels, that the exceeding greatness of the power may be of God, and not from ourselves. We are pressed on every side, yet not straitened; perplexed, yet not unto despair; pursued, yet not forsaken; smitten down, yet not destroyed; always bearing about in the body the dying of Jesus, that the life also of Jesus may be manifested in our body…So then death worketh in us, but life in you. II Corinthians 4:7–10, 12*

I believe the charismatic movement is one of the greatest moves of the Holy Spirit in the history of the church, with all its failings and faults, all its extremes and its excesses. I have no doubt whatsoever that the Holy Spirit was in this whole thing. But I have to say, if I were to talk about being pressed on every side, perplexed, pursued, and smitten down, I reckon most people would think I was a candidate for a deliverance ministry. "Oh, you need to be delivered. Dear brother, this is not the Christian life in fulness. Pressed on every side? No, no, no; haven't you heard of the prosperity gospel? You should be full and overflowing with it. Perplexed? We send people to theological seminaries so they won't be perplexed. You are supposed to have the answers, not be perplexed. Pursued? You should not be pursued. Smitten down?" Phillips put it beautifully in his translation years ago: "Knocked down, but not knocked out."

But that is not what Paul is saying: "Pressed on every side, but not straitened." There is no frustration of the purpose of God, only fulfillment. "Perplexed, yet not unto despair." Always at your wit's end, and the Lord always coming in. "Pursued"—an object for the enemy to pursue —"but not forsaken; smitten down, yet not destroyed; always bearing about in the body the dying of Jesus."

This is a work of the cross that very few believers know much about, if anything. We want to know the power of the Lord, the fulness of the Lord, and the abounding life of the Lord, but we do not want to hear about falling into the ground and dying, or being broken. It is foreign to us. But there is no way for Jacob to become Israel, no way for God to form Israel out of Jacob, unless it is this way. Jabbok—the angel of the Lord wrestled with Jacob all through the night; and at the end of it, Jacob was broken. The old, powerful, devious Jacob was broken and he would never be the same again through his life. He would limp for the rest of his days.

Did Jacob describe this experience as the place of affliction? No! The place of brokenness? No! The place of death? No! The place where God dealt with him? No! He said, "I will call this place Peniel, the face of God." In other words, this is no morgue-like, morbid fascination with suffering and death. It is swallowed up in a discovery of the beauty and glory of the Lord.

Work of the Holy Spirit

It requires exceeding great power to form an Israel out of a Jacob. In Ephesians Paul prays for the saints at Ephesus.

> *That the God of our Lord Jesus Christ, the Father of glory,*
> *may give unto you a spirit of wisdom and revelation*
> *in the knowledge of him; having the eyes of your heart*
> *enlightened, that ye may know what is the hope of his*
> *calling, what the riches of the glory of his inheritance*
> *in the saints, and what the exceeding greatness of his*
> *power to us-ward who believe. Ephesians 1:17–19*

I fear sometime that when we talk about the cross, we miss this, and then a terrible thing happens. I have seen it in so many assemblies and fellowships, companies of God's children. A religious spirit takes over, and everyone becomes heavy and dark and somehow bound. Everyone is frightened to say too much, frightened to do too much, lest it is "me." This is not the cross. The cross frees us. The cross is the most liberating work in the whole world. When that blessed Person of the Holy Spirit takes the work of the cross and applies it to a human life, that human life becomes positive, filled with a new discovery of the Lord in which death is swallowed up in life. You are conscious of death, but everybody else is conscious of life. That is altogether different than when everybody else is conscious of death when they touch you.

When we talk about the exceeding greatness of His power, what are we talking about? We are talking about the exceeding greatness of His power which He wrought in Christ when He raised Him from the dead. It is the Person of the Holy Spirit by whom the Lord Jesus came again from the dead, the Spirit of Him who raised Jesus from the dead (Romans 8). It is the unique work of the Person of the Holy Spirit to form anything. It was He who brooded on the formless, chaotic waters and wastes of the world in the beginning. And when the word of God was spoken, it was the blessed Person of the Holy Spirit who brought order out of disorder and form into formlessness. It has always been the same. It was the Holy Spirit who brought to birth the Lord Jesus, and who at Pentecost formed a body of 120 members out of 120 units of a congregation. It is always the work of the Holy Spirit.

"Fear not, for I have redeemed thee." The Holy Spirit never works apart from the redeeming work of the Lord Jesus. How did you get saved? You thought you signed a decision, or put your hand up, or went forward, or you prayed with somebody; but in actual fact, it was the Holy Spirit who opened your eyes. That day you were first made alive to God, and your eyes opened like a newborn babe to a new world, when you suddenly realized that the Bible that had never meant anything to you before in your whole life now meant something, it was the Holy Spirit who opened your eyes. When you took your first steps in the Christian life, the Holy Spirit empowered you though you hardly knew it. Did you ever weep tears of repentance? The Holy Spirit convicted you. Every time you have seen something more in the work of the Lord Jesus, something more in the Word of God, the Holy Spirit, blessed, gentle, powerful Holy Spirit, opened your eyes. He never works apart from the Lord Jesus, but He is always unveiling the Lord Jesus, always pointing to the Lord Jesus.

Never be afraid of a genuine baptism of the Spirit. To be immersed in the power of the Holy Spirit is a marvelous, marvelous thing. That is what happened to Jacob when he said, this place I shall call the face of God, for I have looked upon the Lord and I have lived (see Genesis 32:30). Anyone who has had a real experience of the Holy Spirit will know what I am talking about. You have to call it the face of God. I saw the Lord. In some new way, in some deeper way, in some fuller measure, I saw the Lord.

Isn't it a marvelous thing that the Lord loves you and loves me so much? And isn't it wonderful that He comes to you and to me and says, "But now thus saith the Lord that created thee, O Jacob, and he that formed thee, O Israel: Fear not, for I have redeemed thee"? The Lord ha a purpose for you. He wants you to be a builder, not a destroyer; a planter, not a supplanter; a blesser and a blessing, not a twister; a worshipper, not a deceiver. That is the purpose of the Lord for you, and it is the purpose of the Lord for me. It is to make us princes with God, people who can reign with Him—that is His purpose. It is so marvelous to know the determination of divine love in this matter. May God bring you to a new discovery of Himself. Above all, may He bring you to an opening up of your own heart to the blessed Person and work of the Holy Spirit, who can lead you in His own inimitable way to your Jabbok and to a seeing of the Lord that will make all the cost worthwhile.

Shall we pray:

Dear Lord, You know our hearts. All of us want to be what You want us to be. We do not want to be anything else. We know, Lord, that only what You do in us is worthwhile. We are living in a world that is topsy-turvy and increasingly so. Lord, while we have time grant that we may know Your wonderful work in our hearts and lives. In some way cast Your Spirit on us so that we are brought to that place where You can do that work in us that will be the conforming of us to the image of Your Son; not in one go, but progressively. We ask it in the name of our Lord Jesus. Amen.

3.
Thou Art Mine By Calling

Isaiah 43:1–2

*But now thus saith the Lord
that created thee, O Jacob, and
he that formed thee, O Israel:
Fear not, for I have redeemed
thee; I have called thee by thy
name, thou art mine. When
thou passest through the
waters, I will be with thee; and
through the rivers, they shall
not overflow thee: when thou
walkest through the fire, thou
shalt not be burned, neither
shall the flame kindle upon thee.*

Philippians 3:4–14

*Though I myself might have
confidence even in the flesh: if
any other man thinketh to have
confidence in the flesh, I yet
more: circumcised the eighth
day, of the stock of Israel, of the
tribe of Benjamin, a Hebrew
of Hebrews; as touching the
law, a Pharisee; as touching
zeal, persecuting the church; as
touching the righteousness which
is in the law, found blameless.
Howbeit what things were gain*

---

to me, these have I counted loss for Christ. Yea verily, and I count all things to be loss for the excellency of the knowledge of Christ Jesus my Lord: for whom I suffered the loss of all things, and do count them but refuse, that I may gain Christ, and be found in him, not having a righteousness of mine own, even that which is of the law, but that which is through faith in Christ, the righteousness which is from God by faith: that I may know him, and the power of his resurrection, and the fellowship of his sufferings, becoming conformed unto his death; if by any means I may attain unto the resurrection from the dead. Not that I have already obtained, or am already made perfect: but I press on, if so be that I may lay hold on that for which also I was laid hold on by Christ Jesus. Brethren, I count not myself yet to have laid hold: but one thing I do, forgetting the things which are behind, and stretching forward to the things which are before, I press on toward the goal unto the prize of the high calling of God in Christ Jesus.

Shall we pray:

Father, when we come to Your word, we must acknowledge in Your presence, and willingly we do so, that without You we can do nothing. I can speak many words, outline truths, but in the end, Lord, it will be to no avail unless You are the ability and the power of this time. And the same with all of us as we listen; we can hear many words, we can hear many truths, but Lord, unless You give us that kind of hearing ear, we shall never hear what You are saying to the churches by Your Spirit. Therefore, Lord, together we avail ourselves of that anointing which You have provided for us, both speaker and hearer. May we together know ability beyond our natural ability, that grace and power of Yours which can enable me to speak Your Word and communicate the burden which is on Your heart, and enable us to hear what it is You are saying and have the grace to obey You. Lord, will You work in our time, delivering it from all futility and vanity? And in the weakness of the physical vessel, let Your power be made manifest. In the name of the Lord Jesus. Amen.

The little phrase that has been so much with me is in Isaiah 43:1: "Thou art mine." I saw in this amazing statement of the Lord through the prophet Isaiah a four-fold way in which we are His. We are His by creation: "But now thus saith the Lord that created thee, O Jacob." The word in Hebrew, *barar,* comes from a root which means "to press something." Actually, it comes from a root "to press into shape." It is an amazing thing when we think of Jacob and his fallen state, in all his twistedness, in all his deviousness, in all his self-will, in the strength of his natural man, that God had created him and he was not a mistake. His temperament, his personality, his genetic history, every single thing about him had been under the sovereign rule of God; and Jacob was not a mistake or an accident that God somehow took up and began to use. The Lord says to Jacob, "I created thee, O Jacob."

Then, we are His by redemption: "And he that formed thee, O Israel: Fear not, for I have redeemed thee." This word, *yatsar,* in Hebrew means "to fashion, to form, to constitute." You may have been pressed into shape; you may have the mold, even though it has fallen and is alienated from God. But the wonderful thing about the redeeming work and grace of God is that He wants to take Jacobs and form them into Israels.

It is a marvelous thing to know that we who are born of God are not only the Lord's by creation, but we are the Lord's by redemption. We are doubly the Lord's. It is a wonderful thing to have been redeemed. The word means in Hebrew, "to free by repayment," or "ransom," or "by avenging." That is exactly what the Lord has done for you and for me. When we had fallen into sin and were alienated from God, we were dead in trespasses and sins, we were in the slave market of the world, demonized in many ways, then our Lord, the Redeemer, came and paid the ransom for us. He avenged us in the sense that He stripped those principalities and powers naked, making a show of them openly, triumphing over them through His cross.

Now, I want to take the third of these ways in which we are His. It is in this word: "I have called thee by thy name, thou art mine." This calling is not the calling to be created. That is obvious. We have to be created to be called. For the calling to operate, we have to be created.

However, we have a much bigger problem when it comes to salvation. Again and again in the New Testament, it seems, superficially, as if this calling is connected with being born again, with being converted, with being saved. But in actual fact, our calling must be more than even our so-great salvation. Our salvation is only the means by which the Lord has retrieved us from our fallen state and brought us into His kingdom.

God's Original Calling for Man

Originally, when God created man, He called man. Man had a calling. What was God's original calling? It was that man should eat of the tree of life. In terms that we understand from the New Testament, it is that man should receive the eternal life of God in the Lord Jesus. He should become joined to Him in one Spirit, and together with the Lord Jesus, they would govern the whole universe. That was the calling. Man fell from it. Because of sin, he fell short of the glory of God.

So our salvation is the means by which God puts us back into the race, puts us back on the course. Although it is true that our calling has very much to do with salvation, it is not a being called to be saved only. It is a calling that becomes operative the moment we are saved because within our salvation is all the grace and the power that you and I need to hear the call of God, to obey the call of God, and to fulfill the call of God. Now if we understand that, we shall begin to see there is a third way in which the Lord claims us when He says, "Thou art mine." We are His by calling; not only by creation, not only by salvation, but also by calling. "I have called thee by thy name, thou art mine."

No wonder the world thinks we are a dreary lot. They think all there is to being a child of God, all that is to do with being saved, is to say a few prayers, sing a few hymns, meet in our rather boring, routine type meetings, witness, if we are very keen, go out on the streets and try to reach a few others, if we are extremely, one hundred per cent committed. Then one day we die; we go into eternity where forever afterwards we will sing in a hallelujah chorus, sit on a damp cloud in a glorified nighty, and play a harp forever and ever. Evidently, this is the gospel as the world sees it. This is the impression we have given to the world, that this is the good news.

But if you could catch even the smallest glimpse of what our calling is, I promise you, it will spoil you forever after. You will never be the same again. You will catch a glimpse of what the goal of your salvation is, what the objective of God's love is, the aim He is driving at. And as you walk with Him, you will begin to see all the many things that happen in your life being turned to work for you an exceeding and eternal weight of glory.

Whether we like it or not, the world is passing inevitably and irreversibly into a time of greater and greater turmoil and upheaval. As we move into this time of monetary collapses, of terrorism, of lawlessness, of nation against nation, of super powers outwitting each other, all the incumbent problems and things that are consequent of it, you and I will become more and more depressed and disappointed, as believers, unless we have caught the heavenly vision. If you and I are people of the heavenly vision, then we shall see all the turmoil and all the upheaval and all the shaking as a blessing in many ways to bring us to priorities, to bring us to understand what we must put first if we are going to have treasure that outlasts time.

Walk Worthily of the Calling

I therefore, the prisoner in the Lord, beseech you to walk worthily of the calling wherewith ye were called. Ephesians 4:1

This is not just a calling, as important and significant as that may be, to some particular function in the body of Christ, to some particular work that the Lord wants to give you, to some particular contribution that you are to make to the house of God, to the church of God. This is, in the most general way, the calling that is ours that becomes operative when you and I are born of God. When we are not born of God, there can be no call. But the moment you and I are born of God, the moment you and I are saved, then inherent within our very salvation is the calling of the Lord. We are told by the apostle Paul to "walk worthily of the calling of the Lord." It is so tremendous, so wonderful, and so eternal in its significance and its dimension. Do not devalue it, do not debase it, do not ignore it, do not live in an unworthy manner in the light of it as if you have not been called; but "walk worthily of this calling wherewith you have been called."

The Hope of His Calling

That the God of our Lord Jesus Christ, the Father of glory, may give unto you a spirit of wisdom and revelation in the knowledge of him; having the eyes of your heart enlightened, that ye may know what is the hope of his calling. Ephesians 1:17–18

How many of us really know what is the hope of His calling? It cannot be salvation surely, in the sense that we are already saved. It could have something to do with the redemption of the body, but is that really the extent of the hope of His calling? Isn't it interesting that the apostle feels he cannot write any more of this letter to the church in Ephesus until he has let them know what he is praying for them? He says, as if he is almost afraid, "I am so afraid you will just mentally understand this as theology. I want the God and Father of our Lord Jesus Christ to give you a spirit of wisdom and revelation in the knowledge of him, the eyes of your heart being enlightened that you may know what is the hope of his calling." There are other things that he prays for them at Ephesus but he puts this first: "What is the hope of his calling. I want you to know that this is the burden of my heart, that you may be given illumination, inward revelation in the knowledge of the Lord Jesus, that you might know what is the hope of His calling. This is going to take you through the periods of tribulation when you will face the wild beasts in the arenas in Ephesus." This is the thing that will enable the church, when it comes to periods of great suffering, to realize that they have a calling, a glorious calling.

Called According to Purpose

> *And we know that to them that love God all things work together for good, even to them that are called according to his purpose. Romans 8:28*

"His" is actually not in the original; and if you think of it for a moment, it brings home the force of the phrase far more. "We know that all things work together for good to them that love God and who are called according to purpose." "Called according to purpose." In other words, there is a purpose in this calling. This calling is not just a haphazard, general thing. You and I are "the called" according to a plan, according to a program, according to a goal that God has for His own. The most general way I can explain this calling is that we are called to be in Christ. You cannot be in Christ unless you are saved, and in Christ you will find your so-great salvation. In Him, you will be saved to the uttermost: from sinner to saint, from Jacob to Israel. It is all in Christ.

Sharing His Destiny

But this calling has much more than even that, in the sense of being called to salvation. If we think of it as being called to be in Christ, then we are called to share His destiny. We are called to share His throne; we are called to share His body; we are called to share His life; we are called to share His name; we are called to share His inheritance; and we are called to share His glory.

We are called to be in Christ. This marvelous little phrase—"in Christ"—is the church. *Ekklesia*—we are called out and called in; we are the called ones, the elect. If we are called to be in Christ, is it possible that we will not share His destiny, we will not share His throne, we will not share His glory? "He that is joined to the Lord is one spirit" (I Corinthians 6:17). How can we be in Christ, joined to Christ, one with Christ, named with the name of the Lord Jesus, given His life, and not share His destiny, His inheritance, His throne, His glory? No, here is your calling.

This is something to knock the world clean out. They think we are such a dreary lot and, unfortunately, we give the impression that we are, especially in our meetings. But the fact still remains that you and I are called with a tremendous calling. I think it is amazing to think that a little Jacob like you and a little Jacob like me have been called to share the destiny of the Messiah. Think of that! You and I—little Jacobs that we are—have been called to share the inheritance of the Lord Jesus. Everything was made through Him and everything was made for Him and in Him everything holds together. And you and I have been called to be in Christ and to share His inheritance. And if we are called to be in Christ, then our calling is to do with the sharing of His destiny, of His throne, of His future, of His inheritance, of His glory.

It is the most wonderful thing in the whole, wide world that through the redeeming grace and love of God, you and I have come to be recipients of the eternal life which is in our Lord Jesus. He said, "I am the resurrection and the life." And you and I, who have been born of God, have the Son, and "he that has the Son has the life." We have this life in us, the very life of the Lord Jesus, the very life of God in the Lord Jesus. It is in me, and it is in you.

Sharing His Name

We share His name. He said to us, "If you come to the Father, ask in My name. Everything you ask in My name, He will give it to you." This does not mean that it is like a little charm. It means that we have been married to the Lord; we have lost our surnames and we have His.

Let me take it a step further: To be in Christ means that you and I are called to be the body of the Lord Jesus. We are called to be joined to Him; and because I am joined to Him and you are joined to Him, we are joined together. We cannot help it. You might not like the idea and I might not like the idea. But the fact of the matter is that you and I, being joined to the one

Lord, are joined to one another. We have different backgrounds, different races, different outlooks, different temperaments, different personalities, but we have only one Lord; and you and I have been called to share in Him.

The Body of Christ

We are His body. Is there anything more intimate than that? I often think how Paul came to use this term, which he uses more than any other, as the illustration of what it means to be the church, the body. When you think about it, it is an extraordinary, awkward thing to talk about people being the body of the Lord, the church, of which He is Head; but we are all so used to it. Some of you have read it from childhood, and it does not seem the least bit awkward. You have known the phrase: "the church which is His body"; or "He is Head of the church, which is His body." But when you think about it, it is very awkward.

What is the point of talking about Jesus as Head and ourselves as body unless we are joined together in a living entity, in a living unity? Have you ever seen a living, bodiless head? Once a head is parted from the body, you can pickle it or you can stick it up on a wall (as they do in some parts of the world in these big, long houses), or you can do something else with it, but it is dead. It has no practical, living function whatsoever. Have you ever seen a living, headless body? I am sure you would die of shock if a headless body suddenly walked down the aisle and sat in the chair. You would have the shock of your life, because you have never seen a living, headless body. For a body to live it has to have a head, and for a head to live it has to have a body. The head and the body belong together; and they can only live in so far as they are joined together in a unity, in an entity.

Do you begin to realize why the Holy Spirit put into the heart of the apostle Paul this illustration of head and body as the unity that is between the Lord Jesus and those whom He has redeemed? He is saying that you belong to Him. You belong to Him in such a way that you cannot live without Him; and although He could live without you, yet He does not want to live without you. That is the glory. You have been given by the Father to the Son; and the Son loves you and me so much that He says He will lose none of those that the Father gives to Him. We are called to be the body of the Lord Jesus.

The Bride of Christ

We are called to be the bride of the Lord Jesus. It is the same thing, in another way, because in the very first chapters of the Bible, it says, "And these two shall become one flesh." When we come to the end of the Bible, there is the Lamb and the wife of the Lamb, and there is the marriage supper of the Lamb. These two finally come together. This is the calling.

When I begin to think of it like this, I understand Paul; I also understand Mr. Sparks. The first time I ever heard Austin Sparks many, many years ago, he prayed at great length before he spoke about the need for us all to have revelation, and I thought he must be nuts. I had never heard a Christian minister or servant of God ever pray that we all need revelation. I thought we had all the revelation we needed in the Bible; all you have to do is use your little brain. So why does he pray that we might all have revelation? Then he gave the word; and afterwards, he prayed again that we might have revelation. And I thought to myself, "No wonder people think he is strange." I had been warned by quite a few to be very careful of him because he is a sheep stealer and he has very strange doctrines. But Mr. Sparks only had the same burden that the apostle Paul had, and when we see what happened to the church shortly after Paul's death, I fully understand why Paul had the burden. It was some kind of intimation in his spirit by the Holy Spirit that unless these people really had revelation the whole thing would go off the rails.

It is no wonder that the apostle, when he had seen something of the calling, prayed, "Oh, that God would give you a spirit of wisdom and revelation in the knowledge of the Lord Jesus, the eyes of your heart being enlightened that you may know what is the hope of His calling." They would be spoilt by anything less than God's highest, fullest, and best. They would be spoilt for all this "playing at churches." They would be spoilt for all this superficial worldliness in the church. They would be spoilt for all this reducing of the house of God to a human club, with all the system of the world, and the organization of the world, the finance-raising techniques of the world, and the electoral procedures of the world. They would understand that this calling of theirs was in another dimension. They would never be the same again. Like the apostle Paul, they would be caught by an obsession; they would have a passion that would spoil them for anything else.

Paul's Obsession

Paul's amazing testimony in Philippians 3 is shattering when you really think of what he said. For instance, he said, "I forget the things that are behind." What is wrong with the man? Most Christians do not forget the things that are behind, and they never even think of the things which are before. Most people are always talking about a blessing they had twenty years ago, or ten years ago, or an experience they had. It is always the past. It is not the way to close the book on the past.

But what has happened to this apostle that he says, "I press on toward the goal to the prize of the high calling of God in Christ Jesus"? Here is this man who has written the Roman letter, the Galatian letter, the first and second Thessalonian letters, and the first and second Corinthian letters, and he says, "I do not count myself yet to have obtained, but I press on." If there is one person in the whole of the family of God that we could say, "He has really got it," it would surely be the apostle Paul. I would give anything to be able to write just 1 Corinthians 15. You would hear about it through all eternity if I had only written that. I would always say, "Did you read what I wrote?" What about 1 Corinthians 13, or Romans 8? Here is this man who has received such great revelation. He has been caught up to the third heaven; he has heard things that are not even lawful for a man to utter; he has had such experiences of the Lord. Yet he says, "I do not count myself yet to have obtained, but I press on."

Then he says, "That I may lay hold on that." *Apprehend* is a very strong word in the Greek. It means to "arrest," the way you take a person into custody. "That I may arrest that for which Christ Jesus arrested me." In other words, when the Lord saved me, He had a purpose, and I want to take hold of that purpose. What was it that was in His heart when He saved me? Why did He persevere with me? Why does He say, "I created you," and then He redeems me even though I am fallen and alienated from God? What is His purpose in creating and redeeming me? Paul says, "I caught a glimpse of it, and I will never be the same again. I do not care whether I go through lions in the arenas, or fight with gladiators in the arenas, or face death in the end by execution, afflictions, shipwrecks, all the privations, or see all my reputation being torn from me, if I can only reach the goal that God has set, if I can only come to the prize of the high calling of God in Christ Jesus." The man is obsessed. One day, in the ages to come, we will never think of Paul as obsessed. We will only say, "Would to God we had all been obsessed!" The man has seen through the things of time and of sense. He has seen through those things that seem to us to be so important as being actually secondary, and he has seen through to that which is eternal, that which abides forever. And he can never be the same again.

He says the most amazing things in this testimony. He says that he counts all things but refuse that he may gain Christ. Now, that is the most unevangelical language I have ever heard. That sounds more like the Catholic tradition than the Protestant tradition—"that I may gain Christ." Actually, it is in the modern version—"that I may win Christ." Now I have to say, "Paul, you do not win Christ. It is wrong for you to use language like this; it is misleading. You do not win Christ; you do not gain Christ. Christ is God's unspeakable gift to you, Paul. What are you talking about, 'counting everything but loss'? You said yourself you are not justified by works. Are you trying to tell us that by letting go of all these things you are going to win Christ, you are going to gain Christ? It is wrong. You are denying and contradicting what you yourself have taught us."

The Prize of the High Calling

Then later on he says, "I count all these things but loss that I may attain unto the resurrection from the dead." What is he talking about? Everybody is going to be raised from the dead anyway. But he uses a very interesting word in the Greek. He says, "That I may obtain to the resurrection which is out from among the dead." What does he mean? It is as if he sees something that God is calling him to. He calls it the prize, and a prize is won. "The prize of the high calling of God in Christ Jesus."

Then he says, "I press on toward the goal to the prize of the high calling of God in Christ Jesus." Evidently, this prize of the high calling of God in Christ Jesus is something for which you and I have got to appropriate the grace and power of God in order to keep on course and run the race and fulfill our ministry until finally, by the grace of God, we reach the finish line. It is not salvation. I personally do not believe that you can lose your salvation, although there are those who do. But I do believe you can lose your position in the city of God because I understand that in many ways the kingdom is bigger than the city.

You will remember, concerning the bride, that it says, "Blessed are those who are invited to the marriage supper of the Lamb." Who are these blessed ones who are invited to the marriage supper of the Lamb? They cannot be the bride since the whole marriage supper is in her honor; and they cannot be the angels because they will be there anyway, attending and serving. So who are the ones who are told that they are so blessed to even be invited to the marriage supper of the Lamb? That leads me to say this about the prize of the high calling of God. I do not believe that Paul is talking about winning the Lord Jesus as Saviour, nor is he talking about winning Him even as Lord; he is talking about winning Him as Bridegroom.

Do you really mean to tell me that our Lord is going to be satisfied with a lot of empty-headed Hollywood stars sitting at His side for all eternity? They are as dumb as they come, but just because they are saved, they are going to sit beside Him! They have never been able to govern their own circumstances, let alone reign over the universe. But because they are saved, evidently they are going to sit on a golden throne next to the Lord. It is nonsense! Even the Lord Jesus was made perfect through the things He suffered. Even the Lord Jesus, who was without sin, sinless, was made complete, was made perfect, was made mature, came to maturity through the things that He suffered.

It is nonsense to talk about inheriting the worlds to come and reigning over them. There is a hedonistic kind of idea of the ages to come—we are all going to enjoy ourselves. We are going to lie around while angels come by with sherbet, and ice cream, and coffee, and tea, and peaches, and plums, and mangoes, and everything. We will not even have to peel an orange because the angel will do it for us. It is going to be absolutely wonderful. It will be flowery beds of ease. You remember the old hymn, "Flowery beds of ease"? It means a flowery bed with all its lovely hangings, and there you will rest on cushions until a bell rings and you will go in for a thousand-year hallelujah chorus. Then you will have another hundred years of eating peaches and ice cream, after which you will go back to lie on your flowery bed of ease. Then you will go out for two hundred, three hundred years, wandering around through the gardens looking at the fountains, looking at the birds, watching the butterflies. Now I know a lot of you think: "I cannot think of anything more lovely. Oh, I cannot wait to get there." You might even be thinking, "You have really gone and done it this time because you have really given me a glimpse of something I want."

But think for a moment. At present you feel weary, you have circumstances that are against you, you have problems of fellowship, and so many other things that are around you. Are you going to tell me that as a human being whom God has created spirit, soul, and body, after thousands and thousands and thousands of years, so to speak, of just sitting around doing nothing, you will not be bored? The human being has been made with a genius for creativity. If we could so measure eternity, which we cannot, you will only be satisfied for a few months of doing nothing. You will be saying, "I would like to do something. I would like to do something."

That is the whole point of what I am trying to say. In these ages to come, God is going to do so much. This universe, this globe, this natural creation, with all its beauty, with all its intricate, complex arrangement and order, is a little shadow of what God really desires. One day, when the whole parenthesis of sin is over and the first things are passed away, God is going to say, "Now, let's get on with the real job. Let's bring new universes into being; let's create new stars; let's do all kinds of things, like watching a tree become something else." I am not being so stupid because it says in Romans 8 that the world has been subjected to a cycle of corruption. So what would God perhaps get out of this? I do not know. But I do know that this world, with all its beauty and fallen state, is the palest, palest, palest, inhibited, bound, caged shadow of what God would have had if there had been no fall. If man had obeyed his original calling, taken the tree of life, received the Lord Jesus, entered into a partnership with the Lord Jesus, and had been glorified and transfigured in glory, then a new phase would have begun. God would have said, "Now, you have looked after the Garden which is the first allotment, now you have conquered the world which was the next allotment, and now we are going to get on with the next job." But we do not know what the next job is. However, if you and I think that we can just sit on thrones, administering the will of God and doing the works of God automatically, we have another think coming.

Very often, the idea about sitting on thrones (especially to those who live in republics) is that the king just sits there with his crown slightly at a tilt, the scepter raised, thinking, "Aren't I wonderful? I hope you are all admiring me in these beautiful robes and wonderful jewels." There were corrupt kings and queens like that, but that is not the real meaning of kingship. The real meaning of kingship is service, and that is what we see in the Lord Jesus. He was the King of the Jews, in whose veins there was nothing but royal blood, even humanly speaking, and who is now King of kings and Lord of lords. He was the suffering Servant. He was the Servant of the Lord.

Training for the Calling

The whole point of this calling is that you and I have got to be trained. If you and I are going to administer the will of God in the ages to come, if we are going to watch over the works of the Lord in the ages to come, we have got to learn now how to walk in step with the Lord, voluntarily, of our own free will, in spite of a world that is against us. We want to be at His side. We choose to be at His side. We are not there because we are frightened of hell; we are there because we want to be, and we are prepared to pay the price to be with Him. That is the kind of person the Lord wants to marry. He does not want people who are there on the throne as His bride who, He knows very well, are only there because they are frightened of hell. Or the only reason they are there is that they want to be admired by others, they want to be popular with the world, they want to be cheered and acclaimed. He does not want that kind of empty-headed arrogance. He wants people who, like Himself, have learned to lay down their lives, who have sacrificed themselves, who have lost their reputations, who have served Him faithfully in humdrum circumstances, who have learned to distinguish His mind in times of great stress and pressure and do His will, and who have loved Him with a first love all the way through. That is why He has called you and me.

The lovely thing about this call is that the Lord calls us, but He does not push us. He calls us; He does not push us. If you do not want to hear that call, if you do not want to obey that call, you do not have to. You will not lose your salvation, you will not lose your place in the family of God, but you will not come to the throne.

The Overcomers

*To the end that ye should walk worthily of God, who
calleth you into his own kingdom and glory." It is
kingdom and glory, kingship and glory, into His own
rule and His own glory. 1 Thessalonians 2:12*

*He that overcometh, I will give to him to sit down with me
in my throne, as I also overcame, and sat down with my
Father in his throne. He that hath an ear, let him hear what
the Spirit saith to the churches. Revelation 3:21–22*

This is very interesting because He does not say this to the whole
church at Laodicea, nor is it to every born again believer; but it is
to him that overcomes. "To him will I grant to sit down with me in
my throne, even as I also overcame and sat down with my Father
in his throne."

*Behold, I stand at the door and knock: if any man hear
my voice and open the door, I will come in to him, and
will sup with him, and he with me. Revelation 3:20*

"If any man hear my voice and open the door ... he that hath an
ear let him hear what the Spirit saith to the churches." In other
words, if you and I are going to realize our calling to the kingdom,
to the kingship, to the sovereign road to the throne and to His
glory, we have to have an ear. Even when the Lord has been
shut out of so much of Christendom, we have to be those who
open the door and say, "Come in." And He will come in and He

will sup with us and we with Him, and to us will be given grace to overcome.

Many Son's to Glory

Whereunto he called you through our gospel, to the obtaining of the glory of our Lord Jesus Christ. II Thessalonians 2:14

And the God of all grace, who called you unto his eternal glory in Christ, after that ye have suffered a little while, shall himself perfect, establish, strengthen you. I Peter 5:10

What a wonderful thing this glory is! No one has really been able to adequately explain or define glory. It is something to do with the manifested presence of the Lord. It is really when God is totally satisfied, then His presence is manifested, and it is glory. Glory is such a wonderful thing. When the Lord Jesus was transfigured in glory, He did not lose anything of His body or His personality or His temperament. It was not like a spotlight coming on Him from above, as many people imagine. But suddenly, an enormous energy was switched on inside of Him and it shone through Him so that every member of His body, and even His clothing, glistened with light. That is what you and I are going to have one day, amazing as it may seem. He is bringing many sons to glory.

We sometimes think of glory as those things that happen with the Queen of England, and all the bands playing. She pins a medal on somebody's chest and all the bands blast out: "Land of hope and glory"; or "Britannia rule"; or something like that. That is not glory. Glory is when something happens, and God is so satisfied and so absolutely at home that, suddenly, it is as if a tremendous energy is switched on in the whole universe. That is what it says at the end of the Bible. That New Jerusalem, the holy city, the wife of the Lamb, the bride of Christ comes down out of heaven, having the glory of God. There is no need of light of sun because the glory of God will light it. Isn't it amazing? This is your calling.

It is worth suffering for this calling. It is worth paying any price for this calling. You will thank me a million times one day. You will say, "Oh, I am so thankful. I went down to that place and I decided there would be no price too big to follow the Lord, no cost too great. I am going to follow the Lord. I am going to obey the Lord. I am going to seek the Lord, with His own, right through to the end."

In Hebrews 9:15 we are told, "We are called to receive the promise of the eternal inheritance."

Do you remember that word in Romans 8:17: "We have been made heirs of God and joint-heirs with Christ"? What does it mean? The Lord Jesus is the heir of all things. He is the rightful heir of all things. It was made through Him, and it was made for Him. He is the heir of the whole universe and everything to do with it and much more, and you and I are joint-heirs with Him. Now that is a calling. Are you going to throw it away so that you can spend millions and millions of years in a divine kindergarten, romping around on the floor? Or are you ready to let God expand you and extend you, cause you to grow, bring you to maturity through the things which you suffer?

Fellowship

God is faithful, through whom ye were called into the
fellowship of his Son Jesus Christ our Lord. 1 Corinthians 1:9

Some of the modern versions very sadly put something like this:
"God is faithful through whom you were called into fellowship
with His Son, Jesus Christ our Lord." I believe we are called into
fellowship with His Son, Jesus Christ our Lord; but the Holy Spirit
said something even more than being called into fellowship with
His Son. He said, "We are called into the fellowship of His Son,
Jesus Christ our Lord."

This city of God at the end of the Bible, this wife of the Lamb is
not one person. It is made up of countless, innumerable saints who
have followed the Lamb down through the ages whithersoever He
went, those who have laid down their lives for His sake and for
the gospel. It is a fellowship; and you and I cannot pursue this
calling, nor can we realize it on our own. If God were to put you
in a Marxist cell, in solitary confinement for the rest of your life,
it may well be that you could not have this fellowship. But you
and I are not in a solitary cell. It is the hardest thing in the world
for us to stay together and to allow God to discipline us and do
the work in us through our brothers and sisters.

We are all looking for the perfect church. Now, if you find a
perfect church, I will come and join it, and it will not be perfect
anymore. We have all got this idea of the perfect church;
we are looking for the perfect church. But there is no such thing as
the perfect church, not down here. The whole idea of the church
down here is like a pressure cooker. Everything is flung in it,

the lid is put down, and it is being cooked. You cannot get out of it. It is a messy business. It is a builder's yard. The building is going up; but everywhere around there are heaps of sand and cement. There are stones over here, chippings here, all the tools of the trade are around. A building site is never a very pleasant thing, but how can you have a house being built without a building site? Nevertheless, everyone wants the building. They are all looking for a perfect building. They forget it says, "Growing up together into a spiritual house to the Lord, being built together, groweth into a holy temple." They are all looking for the house of the Lord, the temple of the Lord, the church, as if it is something absolutely perfect. You will never find it—never! In fact, if you do, it is, without any shadow of a doubt, the sign that it is not the house of the Lord, because there must be something very static about it. If none of the seamy side is being boiled to the surface, something is strange.

Of course, if we could stop anyone being saved, and we could have a little circle of perfect, aged saints who have been battered about and are now beyond gossip, beyond scandal, beyond backbiting, beyond pride, beyond arrogance, perfectly given to the Lord in prayer, in good works and in faith, we would be all right. But suppose the Holy Spirit fell upon us and three thousand were saved? Your perfect little church has suddenly lost its perfection. Suddenly three thousand come in—prostitutes, pimps, drug cases, alcoholics, adulterers, fornicators. The whole lot gets saved and come in. Are you going to tell me that you are not going to have problems? They have got problems in their temperament, problems in their background. Your perfect church is no longer perfect. So, do not pray for anyone to be saved, if you want to stay a little, elite group. Do you see how nonsensical it is?

The fact of the matter is, we need this fellowship of His Son. We have been called into it. That is what the Lord is calling us to, and how can we not have some kind of fellowship with one another down here? How can we not have to come under the authority of other brothers and sisters? How can we not have to know taking responsibility for other brothers and sisters? Somewhere we have to learn something about fellowship down here.

Some of you younger ones may find it very difficult at times. You think, "They are so much older in age." But why do you not just die to yourself and bring in a bit of new life? Just come in and you will find those older folks will start to smile very sweetly after awhile. It is not very easy when you suddenly find someone coming in and asking: "Why do you do it this way? Why do you do it that way? What a strange thing you do."

When I was first saved, I could never understand why, in a group that I went to, they played the organ on Sunday evenings and never played a single instrument at the Lord's Table. I could not understand it, so I asked. I was sent to Coventry for months on end. Nobody ever asked such a question before. Apparently, I should have known that you do not play instruments at the Lord's Table. But I did not know. I was so young, I wanted to find out, so I asked. If you are young in the Lord, do not let the enemy work on you with such propaganda: "Do not give yourself to that fellowship or that group because they are all old and you are young." Maybe without your even realizing it, the enemy is trying to deny your calling and frustrate the purpose of the Lord in your life.

Our Reaction to This Calling

Do you begin to see what an amazing thing this is—His by calling? We are not only His by creation and His by redemption, we are His by calling. We are trebly His. Isn't that marvelous? "I have called thee by thy name." Sometimes we have an idea that the Lord is just calling the whole church in a general way. Anyone who responds will become very precious. It is a general call. It is not true. If you have been saved, He is calling you by name. He has made a provision for you, a provision of grace, and a provision of power, that that calling may be realized, and you may come to obtain the prize of the high calling of God in Christ Jesus.

How are you to react to this calling? First, you must have vision. If you have never, ever seen what the Lord is calling you to, how can you respond? So you must have vision. Secondly, you must get your priorities sorted out. This is the surest way the enemy is going to see that you do not come to obtain the prize of God's high calling in Christ, unless you sort out your priorities. Where is the Lord in your life? Where is the purpose of the Lord in your life? Is it third, fourth, fifth, sixth? Where is it in priority? You have got to get it sorted out. Thirdly, you have got to face the cost. Fourthly, there is an involvement of fellowship. There are others that you have got to find in the Lord if you are going to really come to God's goal. And fifthly, you must have a hearing ear, and you must obey the Lord. If you do not hear what the Lord is saying, it will not be long before you are out of the course.

Many years ago, when I was first beginning to see these things, I asked Mr. Sparks, "Please, tell me, what is an overcomer?"

He looked at me with a twinkle in his eye and he said, "An overcomer is not a perfect person, and he is not even a powerful person; he is someone who is still in the race at the end." I have never forgotten it.

That is an overcomer. If you are going to stay in the race until the end, you are going to have to have an ear that can hear. May God give you a hearing ear to hear what the Lord is saying to you. Amen.

4.
Thou Art Mine By Overcoming

Isaiah 54:11–17

O thou afflicted, tossed with temptest, and not comforted, behold, I will set thy stones in fair colors, and lay thy foundations with sapphires. And I will make thy pinnacles of rubies, and thy gates of carbuncles, and all thy border of precious stones. And all thy children shall be taught of the Lord; and great shall be the peace of thy children. In righteousness shalt thou be established: thou shalt be far from oppression, for thou shalt not fear; and from terror, for it shall not come near thee. Behold, they may gather together, but not by me: whosoever shall gather together against thee shall fall because of thee. Behold, I have created the smith that bloweth the fire of coals, and bringeth forth a weapon for his work; and I have created the waster to destroy. No weapon that is formed against thee shall prosper; and every tongue that shall rise against thee in

judgment thou shalt condemn.
This is the heritage of the
servants of the Lord, and their

righteousness which is of me,
saith the Lord.

Shall we pray:

Heavenly Father, once again as we come to Your word, we want to recognize our absolute dependence upon Thee. Lord, unless You are the anointing grace and power, both for me in my speaking and all of us in our hearing, it will all be in vain. We shall hear words, we shall hear truths, we shall hear doctrines; but Lord, unless You are the One in our midst, the power and the enabling energy of the speaking and the hearing, then it will be to no avail. Dear Lord, by faith we stand into that anointing which is ours through the finished work of our Lord Jesus and made a reality to us in the Person of the Holy Spirit. Heavenly Lord, will You grant us to meet with You that You will be able to deposit something more of Yourself in everyone of us? We ask it in the name of our Lord Jesus. Amen.

The phrase that we have been considering is found in Isaiah 43:1: "Thou art mine." Now I want to consider the last part of this statement in Isaiah 43:2: "When thou passest through the waters, I will be with thee; and through the rivers, they shall not overflow thee: when thou walkest through the fire, thou shalt not be burned, neither shall the flame kindle upon thee." He claims us as His through overcoming. There are rivers to be forded;

there are waters to swim through; there are fires to be endured; there is flame to walk through without it kindling upon us. All this lies between us and the achievement of God's intention and purpose for us as the created, redeemed, and called of God. And the only way that you and I can come to that place of joy, that place of complete fulfillment and total realization, is this path. There is no other way. It is through many tribulations that we enter into the kingdom of God.

Many, many years ago, Samuel Rutherford, in prison in the British Isles, wrote a letter and in it he said: "Men want Christ cheap. They want Him without the cross, but the price will not come down." There is no other way for you and me to reach the throne of God, to become part of the city of God, to be part of the bride of Christ, unless we face the simple fact that there are rivers and waters and fire and flame.

But we do not face these things alone. It is not as if He said: "I am tipping you out; get on as best you can. You have got rivers to ford and waters to swim, fires to walk through and flame, but just see how you can go." He says, "When thou passest through the waters, I will be with thee." So, this is not a question of being "tipped out" to overcome the best we can. This is learning how to overcome by keeping in step with the Overcomer, the One who is already the victor. He is the key to our overcoming.

Three-Fold Cord

The Savior

The theme of overcoming is the most realistically practical theme, other than our salvation, in the whole Bible. There is a three-fold cord that runs right through the Bible from Genesis to Revelation; and wherever you turn, you will find it. The first strand, and the most important strand, is the Person of the Lord Jesus—the Savior, the Messiah, the King, the Redeemer. You will find Him on every page from Genesis all the way through to Revelation. There is not a page in the Bible that you will not find the Lord Jesus. He is there all the way through the Bible, from beginning to end.

The Church

The second strand is intimately linked with, and twined around, the first strand. You will never find the second strand apart from the first strand; and the second strand is the redeemed people of God. Everywhere you look, on every page, from Genesis all the way through to the book of Revelation, you will find the object of God's love. It is not only the Lord Jesus whom the Father has set His love upon and has purposed that all things shall come to Him, but a people that He is creating through the work and Person of the Lord Jesus. Wherever you look in the whole Bible, you will find the church. It is in picture form in Noah and the seven other members of his family in the ark. It is in Abraham and his family. It is in the nation that is produced in Egypt. It is in the people of Israel as they go over into the land to possess it. It is in the New Testament as you come to the realization of the fulfillment of so much in the gathering out of the church, the coming of the Holy Spirit, and the manifestation of the body of the Lord Jesus. All the way through the whole Bible, you will find this marvelous picture of the church, the redeemed people of God. They are everywhere.

When you come to the end of the Bible, it is the LAMB, the LAMB, the LAMB. He is the glory of this city, and the nations walk in the light of that glory. We discover that it is not just the Lamb alone, but it is the wife of the Lamb, it is this holy city, this New Jerusalem, this bride of Christ joined to the Lord Jesus. That is what we come to when we come to the end of the Bible. It is all the way through from beginning to end. It was always the purpose of God to use the church to glorify the Lord Jesus, just as it was through the Lord Jesus that the church was produced. It was the purpose and design of God that the church, as the body of Christ reaching out all over the earth, should be the means for holding the testimony of Jesus amongst the nations so that men and women could come to know God through and in our Lord Jesus.

The Remnant

That is where we come to the third strand because wherever we look in the Bible, from Genesis to Revelation, we find that the people of God have failed. It sounds horribly negative, but most of us have lived long enough amongst the Christians to know the truth of it. We have no sooner touched the glory of the Lord, and the power of the Lord, and the life of the Lord than we begin to fail. We break up, we divide, factions arise, and error comes in; all kinds of things happen. So you have the third strand, the overcomer. All the way through from Genesis to Revelation, we discover that God takes a remnant of His people—sometimes so small there is only one person, sometimes just a family, sometimes just a few, sometimes more than a few—and He uses the remnant to fulfill the purpose He had for the whole. So at the end of the Bible, even when the majority have failed, His purpose concerning the Lord Jesus is fulfilled by the remnant that have been faithful by His grace.

Abraham

Let's take a very quick ramble through the Bible in this whole question of the overcomer, and we will start with Shem. Shem had many other sons, not only the Messianic line, and they failed. When we come to Ur of the Chaldees, we find they are scattered everywhere, all over the place. Then He takes one man. The God of glory appeared to Abraham and He said, "Get thee out of thy father's house and out of thy kindred, out of Ur of the Chaldees into a place that I will show you." It is the remnant again. The majorities have failed, and God takes hold of the one to fulfill His purpose.

Later on, we have a whole family that number at least seventy. There is every kind of trouble in this family. There is rivalry, jealousy, immorality, rape, fornication, lying, deviousness, murder. If ever there was someone who learned through his family what he was like, it was Jacob. He never realized his own nature until he saw himself in his own sons.

Joseph

Then, the Lord takes Joseph, and He gives this one a dream. We would have said, "That was very unwise, Lord; You should not have given him that dream. You made him so big-headed. He saw all these stars and the sun and the moon bowing down. Then he saw all these sheaves, and they all bowed down to his sheaf. It is enough to make anyone big-headed." But the Lord was taking one member of the family, Joseph, to save the whole family;

and the rest turned against that one member of the family. They sold him into slavery, and he was taken down into Egypt. There, he went down into Pharaoh's dungeon. Iron entered into his soul and he was left there, rotting, while the word of the Lord tried him, until the Lord's time came for him to be taken out and given the supreme place of power and authority in the whole Egyptian empire. God used Joseph, not only to save the Egyptians, but to save his own family. Otherwise, there would not have been a Messianic line. Just as God had taken hold of Abraham, now He takes hold of Joseph and saves that line for His own purpose, that He might fulfill His purpose through the few, for the whole.

A Nation

Later on, we find a whole nation has been produced in Egypt. In spite of the fury and anger of the powers of darkness through the pharaohs and the murder of the Jewish boys at birth, they have multiplied and multiplied and multiplied. Then, the Lord takes them out. He hears their groaning and their cries and tears. He says: "I will come down; I will save them. I will redeem them with a mighty hand and an out-stretched arm. I will take them out of Egypt." He judged Egypt with ten great plagues until, in the end, Pharaoh said, "Go."

When they were out, God revealed Himself to them and finished the whole of Pharaoh's army. Almost immediately, they began to complain and murmur. They talked of stoning Moses and Aaron, saying they wanted to go back to Egypt, that it was better in Egypt. And the Lord said, "What can I do with My purpose? This people that I formed for Myself, this people that is going to be the vessel of My salvation to the ends of the earth—look at them." What happened? A whole generation died in the wilderness, but not in negativism. No, not at all. They had the pillar of cloud by day and the pillar of fire by night. They heard the thunderings of the Lord's voice in the mount. They saw the tabernacle set up. They saw the water come out of the rock. For those forty years, they saw the manna come every day, except the Sabbath. They were able to collect on Friday what we call Erev Shabbat. They were able to collect two portions that day to take them over the Sabbath. Their feet never swelled; think of that! The soles of their sandals never wore out; think of that! Their clothes never wore out in forty years! Has it ever occurred to you they had no tailors, nor did they have any cloth? Where would they spin the stuff in the wilderness? It is so amazing! Here were these people who had angered the Lord and were going to fall in the wilderness because the Lord had said they could not go into the Promised Land to the place where He had caused His name to dwell. Yet, there was no negativism.

This is so much like the Christianity we know. When we begin to see something, we like to devalue Christianity. We say: "Oh, it is nothing, all of that evangelism, all of those big meetings, and healings. Don't you know all the money that is bound up? It is nothing." We like to devalue it all. The Lord never devalues it. The Lord goes on leading, the Lord goes on saving, the Lord goes on healing, the Lord goes on providing; but they will not inherit. They have turned away from their so great calling. But the Lord takes a new generation of children; and that is the generation of another spirit that will go over into the land. So the great purpose of God to bring the Messiah to the earth is going to be fulfilled.

Once again, we see the same principle: the majorities fail and God takes up a remnant.

Gideon

In the time of Gideon the land had so many Midianites, Girgashites, all the "ites," Philistines, all kinds, everywhere around them. It seemed as if they came from every corner to sit on God's people. Then the great army of thirty-two thousand rallied itself to Gideon. "We will do it. Leave it to us." And the Lord said to Gideon, Do they think they are going to beat all these 'ites'? Take them down to the spring in Harod and tell everyone who is a little bit afraid, 'If you want to go home, you can go home.'" Twenty-two thousand went home. I can imagine some of those close to Gideon saying, "Gideon, this is a terrible mistake, a stupid mistake. Twenty-two thousand have gone. You know the camels of the Philistines and Midianites are like the grains of sand on the seashore, let alone the people. What are we going to do?" And Gideon said, "That is all right, we have got ten thousand. They are the best." And the Lord said, "What did you say? Ten thousand? No, no, no, that is too many." "Too many, Lord? What are You going to do?" In the end, Gideon ended up with three hundred; and the Lord used the three hundred to overcome all the Midianites and the Philistines and drive them out of the land. It is the same thing all over again.

David

When Saul is made king and has the whole kingdom, it seems as if it is absolute. God says, "This man is flesh. He will never inherit My kingdom." Then He does not take the finest of

Jesse's sons, the six foot-four ones with broad shoulders and bulging muscles. Samuel, by the Lord, keeps on saying to Jesse, "There must be another." Jesse says, "How many have you seen now?" He has gone through them all except David. "David is the darling of our family, but he is only a kid. He is a cheeky kid, too. He will be a good, strong man one day; but he is only a kid." Samuel says, "Let me see him." So Jesse sends one of his servants out to find David. "There is someone to see you, David." When David comes in, Samuel says, "That is the man." I think Jesse nearly dropped dead. He says, "All my sons—great, big, strapping fellows—and you take this youngest boy of the lot?" Samuel says, "Let me anoint him. This is the man after God's own heart. This is the man who is going to inherit the kingdom and whose name will go through to the very end connected with the Messiah who is to come—Son of David." It is the same principle again.

The Exiles

It is the same principle when all the children of God are taken into exile and they have settled down to a very comfortable life in the exile (and they did have a comfortable life). One of the wonderful things about living in Israel is all our latest research. Because we have a three to four-thousand-year history as a people, we now have people investigating every single aspect of our history. Some of the most interesting things we discover now are what it was like to live in Babylon when they were exiled under Nebuchadnezzar. Very swiftly, the Jewish folks had gotten the banking system, the postal system, and much of the commerce in their hands. And in this marvelous, great metropolis of Babylon, they had wonderful homes. They felt they had a much more pure form of worship. They had no temptation anymore to worship idols, now that they were in the seat of idolatry. They had the synagogue where they went to pray, to worship, and study the word of God together.

But the Lord said, "How will it be possible for My purpose to be fulfilled if all My people remain in exile? They can worship Me. It is true they abhor idolatry now, and they are purer than they have ever been since I took them out of Egypt." But what about the prophetic word of Isaiah:

But thou, Galilee of the nations ... Unto us a child is born, unto us a son is given; and the government shall be upon his shoulder: and his name shall be called Wonderful, Counselor, Mighty God, Everlasting Father, Prince of Peace. Isaiah 9:1b, 6

It is connected with Galilee and the way of the sea, but there was no Galilee. Galilee had been destroyed. All the towns and villages had been devastated.

What about the prophet Micah who had already prophesied at that point,

But thou, Bethlehem Ephratah, which are least among the thousands of Judah, out of thee shall come forth he that shall be ruler of my people, Israel, whose goings have been from old, from everlasting Micah 5:2

But how could He come out of Bethlehem? There was no Bethlehem. It had been razed to the ground, and the whole population had been exiled.

Then, a tiny remnant of the millions in exile, almost sixty-six thousand people, in three waves, went back to the land. Sixty-six thousand—no wonder everyone laughed about it. No wonder everyone thought, "What is this?" But they went back to the land and they rebuilt Jerusalem, they rebuilt Bethlehem, they rebuilt the towns and villages of Galilee. And they repopulated the land so that, in the end, the whole great dispersion, all the people in exile, came into the blessing of the coming of the Messiah.

Birth of the Church

In the New Testament, there is the same thing. There is all the work of the Lord Jesus, the ministry of the Lord Jesus, and finally, the work of the Lord Jesus on the cross—His death, burial, and resurrection. Then there is His ascension and the pouring out of the Holy Spirit, and the whole thing began. Suddenly, one hundred and twenty members of a congregation became one hundred and twenty members of a body, and the whole of Jerusalem was turned upside down. Then all the towns in Judea were turned upside down, and it went into Samaria and they were turned upside down. Finally, it got to Caesarea, into a Gentile Roman officer's drawing room and a meeting packed with Gentiles. It was the beginning of the great Gentile evangelistic mission of the church, which was the most successful evangelistic mission ever launched by the church. That is why you are all here today. You are all the result of that little drawing room meeting in a Gentile Roman officer's home in Caesarea that Peter addressed, and the Holy Spirit fell upon the Gentiles, and they were saved and brought into the family of God.

But we do not have to go very far before we begin to find things are not so good. We find that there are things like Nicolaitanism; and the Lord says, "This thing I hate." He spoke to the church at Ephesus, which was one of the very best: "Repent or I will remove your lampstand out of its place. You have left your first love." To another church He said that there was a Jezebel teaching the deep things of Satan. The Laodicean Church had become so affluent, so knowledgeable; it had so arrived, in its own estimation, that it did not need the Lord. He was knocking outside the door. He is the Head of the church; He is the Saviour of the body; He is the One who has constituted the church; He is the builder of the church; and in His own church, He has been shut out.

> Behold, I stand at the door and knock: if any man hear
> my voice and open the door, I will come in to him, and
> will sup with him, and he with me. Revelation 3:20

The Overcomer

Now you begin to understand why the Lord has one message and one message only to these seven churches, which either represent, as some people believe, the whole church in this age or represent seven local churches symbolizing the whole church on earth and in time. There is one single message to every one of these churches: "To him that overcomes will I grant ..." this and this and this. "To him that overcomes ..." "To him that overcomes..." "To him that overcomes ..." "To him that overcomes ..." Seven times the Lord says it to every one of these churches. Before the veil is ever drawn aside and we see the whole course and purpose of God through this age, we see persecution, dragons, serpents, great world-wide systems symbolized by the figure 666, false prophets, antichrists; we see all these terrible things. We see a false, prostitute church riding on the back of this Babylon called "mother of mysteries—the harlot." Before the curtain is even drawn aside, the risen Lord, in the midst of seven churches, says: My dear ones, the only way I am ever going to fulfill My purpose will not be through the majority, unfortunately, but through the remnant. "To him that overcomes ..." "To him that overcomes ..." "To him that overcomes ..."

And when we come to the last chapters of the book of Revelation, they are almost introduced with these words:

He that overcometh shall inherit these things; and I will be his God, and he shall be my son. Revelation 21:7

We must be careful we do not take this too far, but a son is more than a baby. A baby cannot take over the family business; a son can. A baby is a baby; it is precious, loved, and named with the name of the family, but it cannot, at that age take over the family business. However, a baby can grow up, and he is a son to the end of his days. When he grows to maturity, he can take over the whole family business.

"He that overcomes shall inherit these things." What are "these things"? They are the city, the bride, the new heaven and the new earth wherein dwells righteousness. "He that overcometh shall inherit these things. I will be his God and he shall be my son."

What is an overcomer? I cannot think of any teaching that has, sometimes, been more horribly abused and misused than the teaching of the overcomer because people have gotten the idea that overcomers are elite. They think if you just hear this teaching, you are an overcomer; or if you belong to a particular group, you are an overcomer. I am sorry, but it is not true. The Lord never said, "To those that are overcomers." He said, "To him that overcomes." It is within the context of the whole that we overcome, and it is in relation to our other brothers and sisters that we overcome.

An overcomer is a survivor. When we speak about burnt-out veterans, it is a question of how burnt out you are. If you are totally burnt-out, you cease surviving.

However, an overcomer is not just a survivor; that would be to devalue the whole thought and significance of the overcomer. But there is within it something like that. Are you still in the race? Then, by the grace of God, you are an overcomer. Are you still on the course? Then, by the grace of God, you are an overcomer. Have you been knocked out, fallen out of the race, absolutely puffed out? Then, you are finished. An overcomer is more than a survivor; he is a victor. By the grace and power of the Lord he obtains the victory.

One thing that Mr. Sparks said many, many years ago, delivered this whole matter of overcoming for me: "The overcomer is not an elite, superior group that looks down upon all other believers because they feel they have something the rest do not have. The overcomer is an advance, working party. They are the working party sent ahead of the others to do all the dirty work so that the rest come into the blessing." Now, I do not know how far we can take that, but it certainly delivers this whole idea of elitism, of superiority. It brings it back to the heart of the matter.

Those who lay down their lives for the rest— that seems, to me, to be the overcomer.

The City—The Bride

I want to take this a step further. In Revelation 21 and 22, we have this vision of the city and the bride. How amazing it is that we have these two, quite different ideas wedded in one entity! I have never heard of a bride described as a city, and I have never heard of a city described as a bride. We would all think a man was crazy if he said, "This is my wife, my city." Therefore, we have to take note of this extraordinary wedding of two quite different ideas: the bride—suggesting love, intimacy, union, fellowship; and the city—suggesting government, administration, commerce, empire. We have the two things wedded into one; and we are told that this city, in which the throne of God is forever and ever, is the bride of the Lord, the bride of Christ. This city, this bride, is made up of overcomers. No one who is part of that city or that bride is not an overcomer. Everyone who makes up the bride and the city is, by the grace of God alone, an overcomer. They have possessed what they were called to. They have realized their calling, and they have fulfilled their calling. They have reached the goal, the prize of the high calling of God in Christ.

The Materials for the Building

This bride, this city, is produced out of only three materials—gold, precious stone, and pearl. There is no other material in this bride, no other material in this city. From top to bottom, from side to side, it is produced out of gold, refined as crystal, transparent as crystal; precious stone that has been worked into twelve great foundation layers upon which the city is built; and pearl that has been worked into twelve gates. In the Bible, these three materials stand for one thing only. They stand for or symbolize the nature and life and excellencies of the Lord Jesus. Gold is always symbolic of the divine nature. Precious stone is always symbolic of the excellencies of the nature of the Lord Jesus, perfected through sufferings. The pearl is the deepest and most profound form of suffering of all. The interesting thing is that God has to produce those materials in you and me in one, short life. If you and I are going to be part of that city, part of that bride, then God has got to produce in me and you, in Jacobs, the gold of His life and nature, the precious stone of His excellencies, and the pearl of the fellowship of His sufferings.

Rivers–Waters–Fire–Flame

The Lord spoke to the church in Laodicea in Revelation 3:18: "I counsel thee to buy of me gold refined by fire."

If the Lord had not said this, we would have a real problem about it because, surely, we would say this gold is God's unspeakable gift to us; we cannot buy it. What did the Lord mean about buying the gold of His life? We receive His life through the grace of God. How then are we to buy it? The price is experience— rivers, waters, fire, flame. How is God going to produce in me the gold of His nature? How is God going to produce in me the precious stone of the life and nature of the Lord Jesus? How is He going to produce a pearl in me? Rivers, waters, fire, flame. In waters and rivers, we find gold and we find pearl. In Genesis 2, there is a mysterious little word that says, "If you follow the river, you will come to the land of Havilah, and in this land you will find gold, and the gold is good." So what is God saying? Waters, rivers—gold and pearl. How is precious stone formed? It is formed by intense heat and pressure through fire and flame.

What is God saying to us? There is a cost attached to fulfilling the calling; there is a price to pay. The path to the city lies through fire and water. There is no other way for anyone to become part of the bride, no other way for you to be built up into the city, except through fire and through water. The material is to be produced in our life, and the horrifying thing is that we have only one, short life in which all those materials can be produced. Many of us have already thrown away one-half or two-thirds of that one, short life playing at church, paddling around in superficiality, being contented with a compromised, worldly, spiritual life.

In the ages to come, if we have paid the price and let the Lord lead us through the waters, the rivers, the fire, and the flame, we shall thank Him on bended knees, with tears running down our faces, that He led us through such a way to obtain the glory that has come to us in Christ. Do you think any one of us will say, "Oh dear, what a price we suffered!" When we are in the glory of the Lord, the eternal glory of God in Christ, when we are enjoying the eternal inheritance, when we are sharing the throne with the Lord Jesus, when we have that intimate union with Him, do you think any one will talk about the afflictions, the tribulations, the sacrifice, the cost, or the price? We will say it was all the grace of God, the grace of God, the abounding grace of God that took us through rivers and waters and turned the rivers and waters into the producing of gold and pearl. We shall thank God. If I may put it like this: we shall kiss His feet, we shall weep at His footstool and say, "Lord, thank You, thank You, thank You, that You took us through those rivers and waters, that You took us through those fires and flame." In the waters, the gold was produced; in the waters, the pearl was formed; in the fire, the precious stone was produced. "Thank You, Lord." It is the Spirit of the Lord dwelling in us and coming upon us, Who enables us to turn all these things to eternal value.

Light Affliction—Eternal Glory

We have made such a misery of the Christian life: "Oh dear, it is such a hard business being a Christian. We are against the tide, going against the current. It is so difficult to be a Christian." But if we only had the vision of the apostle Paul, we could say,

> *Our light affliction which is but for a moment has worked for us, an eternal and exceeding weight of glory.* II Corinthians 4:17

"Oh," you say, "my circumstances are far worse. I would like to put the apostle Paul in my home with ten screaming children and a husband that is no good, or put him in my office where everything goes wrong all the time, or put him in my fellowship where everyone is at sixes and sevens. I do not know what you are talking about."

This is what Paul called light affliction: he was stoned, beaten three times with thirty-nine stripes, left for dead at least twice, shipwrecked once, and spent four years, at least, in prison. I do not know whether I would consider it light affliction. These days, most people would have written a book or two on it. But isn't it a question of what standard of values you are using? If your life is bounded by the things of time and sense, it is not light affliction. It is total affliction, consistent affliction, tribulation without end; and it is making your whole life a misery. "I have only got one, short life. Why should I have all these troubles?" But if you look through to the eternal, then you will thank God, because in the waters that He is leading you through, you will find the gold and the pearl. And the rivers will not overflow you. Sometimes you will only have your nose above water; but still, you will come through. And when you walk through the fire you will not be burned and neither will the flame kindle upon you. You will not lose anything. We are all afraid of fire because of what we will lose in the fire. You will not lose anything that is of value in the fire. You will neither be burned nor will the flame kindle upon you. This is the path of the overcomer. There is no other path.

Many of God's servants down through the ages have come to the place where, in some river that should have overflowed them, they have instead found the gold or the pearl. I think of George Matheson. When he was a young man in the church of Scotland, he was so "all out" to serve the Lord. He needed a bride at his side in the work. He had a childhood friend who had been saved at the same time as he. It just seemed as if everything was going to be beautiful. Then one day, he had some trouble reading the Scripture. He went to the doctor, and the doctor sent him to a specialist. The specialist said, "I am very sorry, Mr.

Matheson, but you are going to lose your sight within six months."
When he went back to his fiancée, within a week she had cooled
off, broken the engagement, and walked out of his life. He had
nothing, except that he knew God had called him. On the day she
married another man, he went to his study and wrote the hymn:

O love that wilt not let me go,
I rest my weary soul in Thee;
I give Thee back the life I owe,
That in Thine ocean depths its flow,
May richer, fuller be.

O Cross, that liftest up my head,
I dare not ask to fly from Thee,
I lay in dust life's glory, dead,
And from the ground there blossoms red,
Life that shall endless be.

Gold, precious stone, pearl. One day, George Matheson will
thank God that he lost his bride because he discovered gold
that is forever.

I think of Amy Carmichael, her great work, and the way the
Lord used her to salvation. So many marvelous things were
happening in that southern part of India. Then one day, they
went to look at an extension of the work. When they got there,
the man who should have come with the key did not come on time,
and they could not find the key. Finally, when he came, the tropical
dusk had fallen. When he put the key in the gate and opened the
door, nobody knew that on the other side of the door coolies

had dug a trench, six feet deep and four feet wide, that should not even have been there. They all stood aside to let "Amma," as they called her, step in first. She stepped in, fell into the trench, and broke her hip, her ankle, and her arm. They dragged her out, put her in the jeep, and drove her fourteen or more miles over rough roads to a makeshift hospital where they set her leg. They said to her: "Don't worry. In a few months you will be as right as rain and back in the work." On her sick bed, she wrote the first of her books and entitled it, *"Rose from Brier"*. In her book she said: "I am just here for a little while. But God has shown me so much through my being put on my back, that I want to share it with others." She little knew that she was going to be on her back, immobilized, for twenty-seven years. But out of that terrible, inexplicable thing came a ministry to the suffering amongst God's people that is unparalleled in the whole history of the church. I find there are no other books like the books of Amy Carmichael that I can give to those who have inexplicable sufferings. She found pearls.

I think of Mr. Sparks who was, as I knew him, such a warm man. Most people thought of him as so austere and so distant, almost royal; but when you knew him, he was a very warm man who could laugh and joke. The one thing, humanly, that he always wanted was acceptance; and the one thing that he never got throughout his ministry was acceptance. Rejected, rejected, rejected and rejected, again and again and again. But in it all, through the rivers he went through and the waters that he passed through, and the flame and the fire, he discovered gold and pearl and precious stone.

It does not matter where we turn in our own generation, we see these things. I think of dear Brother Nee, for twenty years in solitary confinement. Wasn't that a river? Wasn't that water? Wasn't that fire? Wasn't that flame? Why did the Lord keep him alive for twenty years in solitary confinement to take him at the end? Why such waste? But it was not waste—in the rivers, gold; in the waters, pearl; in the fire and the flame, precious stone. At the end, it is all in the city; it is all in the bride.

The Unfailing Promises of God

There are two more things I just want to underline, literally. The first thing I want to underline or point you to is what I have already mentioned, the divine and unfailing promise: "When thou passest through the rivers, I WILL BE WITH THEE." That is the divine, unfailing promise. He said: "Go and make disciples of all nations, and lo I am with you always, even to the end of the age." It is the promise of the Lord that is so glorious: "I will be with thee." Then, think of the discoveries we are going to make. In the river, we find He is with us; in the waters, we discover He is there. That is why they cannot overflow us.

I always used to say that those disciples in that boat were in the safest place on earth when our Lord was asleep in the boat. I would rather have a sleeping Christ in the boat than a wide-awake, unsaved captain. Supposing it had gone to the bottom, they would have had another experience of being raised, wouldn't they? They would have had a wonderful experience. In fact, I have often thought that perhaps they would have learned to walk on the water long before Peter did. Even if they lost the boat, they could not lose their lives, not with the Master of all creation in the boat with them.

When He says, "I will be with thee," He will be with you. If He is leading you, it does not matter where, do not be afraid. The river is meant for your blessing. Do not just see it as some great, evil, dark, terrible circumstance, some great affliction and tribulation. Look upon it as the means by which more gold is going to be produced in your life and more pearl and more precious stone.

Have you noticed another lovely thing? "When thou passest through the waters, I will be with thee and through the rivers, they shall not overflow thee; when thou walkest through the fire, thou shalt not be burned, neither shall the flame kindle upon thee." Did you notice that one little word: THROUGH, THROUGH, THROUGH? You are not meant to permanently dwell in the river. You are not meant to be "at sea" all the time. You are not meant to be living in the fire, in the furnace. It is through, and "I will be with you." And as you walk through it, you are obtaining something that, one day, is going to be the substance for glory.

The Finished Work

When the rivers have been crossed, the waters have been swum through, the fire and the flame have been endured, the end of it all is that the bride has made herself ready; the city is built up; the whole work is done; it is completed. That leads me to these wonderful words of the Lord in Isaiah 45: "I will give thee the treasures of darkness, the hidden riches of secret places." He goes on to talk about Jacob and Israel, "Whom I have called. I have called thee by thy name. You are mine." Or, I think of these other wonderful words in Isaiah 54: "O thou afflicted, tossed with tempest, and not comforted, behold, I will lay thy foundations with fair colors." Then He goes on to describe the sapphires and the rubies and the carbuncles and "all thy borders of precious stones and the peace of your children shall be great, and those that oppress you will be far away."

We began by talking about Jacob, and Israel being formed out of Jacob. And when we come to the end, to our amazement, we find that the old, twisted, devious, supplanting Jacob has become an overcomer. I see him in my mind's eye, old and white-haired, bent and broken, with the beauty of the Lord our God upon him, shining out of his eyes, shining through that old face of his that had seen so much sorrow and so much suffering. It is the glory of the Lord. Jacob has finally become pure in heart. He is going to see the Lord's face, he is going to serve Him, and the Lord is going to write His name on his forehead. Dear Jacob has become a blesser. We see him there on his death bed. It is a beautiful scene in Genesis 48 and 49 when he lifted his hands, he put them on the boys, and he said, "Lord, bless the lads." The two boys were so young they came out from under the legs of Joseph. This is no trite "God bless you." This is a blessing that is with us to this day. Jacob blessed his twelve sons in the end with such insight, with such understanding, that we have it to this day as an understanding. He had become a worshiper. If God can do it with Jacob, He can do it with you and me. It is the God of Jacob Who is the key to the formation of Israel out of Jacob.

It would be marvelous enough if God only formed Israel out of Jacob; but He called Jacob. Can you imagine that? This devious, twisted man, who only ever took and never gave—God called him with an on-high calling. He called this Jacob to His eternal glory, to obtain, to receive the eternal inheritance. That is where I get my comfort because if God can do it with Jacob, He can do it with me."

And here I am. I have gone through some rivers and some waters, and I have gone through some fire. I suspect there are many more rivers and waters to go through, and a good deal more fire to pass through. But I think to myself: "If God has made available to me His grace and His power, I will not turn back. I must go on, forgetting the things which are behind, I will press on toward the mark, toward the goal, to the prize of the high calling of God in Christ." It is worth it because for every river there is gold, for all the water there is more pearl, for all the fire and flame there is precious stone. If I were to accumulate all these things here, I would have to leave them all when I die; but this is forever. That throne of God, that bride of Christ, has been placed in a vessel that is eternal, that is forever.

Dear people of God, may the Lord call you in a way that you have never understood before, and may He give you a glimpse of that overcoming life. It does not mean that you will never know weakness, or failure, or sin; not at all. But it does mean that by His grace and by His power, you will go on and on and on like Jacob until, finally, God has realized and fulfilled His purpose for you.

Shall we pray:

Lord, You know that we all feel in some measure like Jacob. But we are so thankful that You have called even Jacob to Your eternal glory, and You have provided all the grace and all the power for Jacob to become Israel. Lord, we want to thank You and we pray that in some way, You will get Your word right into us. None of us like suffering or affliction. But Lord, if we can see it swallowed up in life, if we can see it as that which You will use to produce more and more of that eternal and exceeding weight of glory, then we want to go with You the whole way. We want to commit ourselves to You, whatever the cost, so that Lord, You can do the work in us You long to do. Oh, heavenly Father, every one of us is a potential part of that city, a potential member of the bride. We pray that not one of us will come short, not one of us, Lord, will turn aside. But may we be those who take hold of Your grace and power and will know that overcoming life of Yours that will bring us, finally, into Your presence with exceeding joy. Lord, we give to You all the praise and all the glory. Write this matter on our hearts; we pray in the name of our Lord Jesus. Amen.

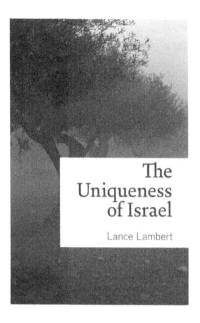

The Uniqueness of Israel

Woven into the fabric of Jewish existence there is an undeniable uniqueness. There is bitter controversy over the subject of Israel, but time itself will establish the truth about this nation's place in God's plan. For Lance Lambert, the Lord Jesus is the key that unlocks Jewish history He is the key not only to their fall, but also to their restoration. For in spite of the fact that they rejected Him, He has not rejected them.

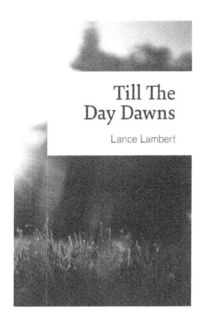

Till The
Day Dawns

Lance Lambert

Till the Day Dawns

"And we have the word of prophecy made more sure; whereunto ye do well that ye take heed, as unto a lamp shining in a dark place, until the day dawn, and the day-star arise in your hearts." (II Peter 1:9).

The word of prophecy was not given that we might merely be comforted but that we would be prepared and made ready. Let us look into the Word of God together, searching out the prophecies, that the Day-Star arise in our hearts until the Day dawns.

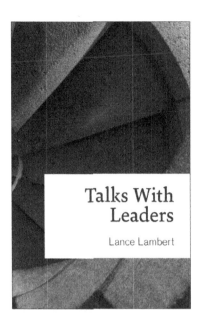

Talks With Leaders

"O Timothy, guard that which is committed unto thee ..." (1 Timothy 6:20) Has God given you something? Has God deposited something in you? Is there something of Himself which He has given to you to contribute to the people of God? Guard it. Guard that vision which He has given you. Guard that understanding that He has so mercifully granted to you. Guard that experience which He has given that it does not evaporate or drain away or become a cause of pride. Guard that which the Lord has given to you by the Holy Spirit. In these heart-to-heart talks with leaders Lance Lambert covers such topics as the character of God's servants, the way to serve, the importance of anointing, and hearing God's voice. Let us consider together how to remain faithful with what has been entrusted to us.

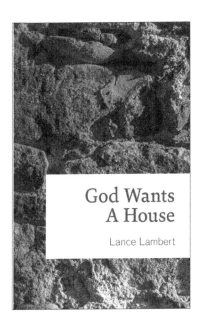

God Wants
A House

Lance Lambert

God Wants a House

Where is God at home? Is He at home in Richmond, VA?
Is He at home in Washington? Is He at home in Richmond, Surrey?
Is He at home in these other places? Where is God at home?
There are thousands of living stones, many, many dear believers
with real experience of the Lord, but where has the ark come
home? Where are the staves being lengthened that God has finally
come home? In God Wants a House Lance looks into this desire of
the Lord, this desire He has to dwell with His people. What would
this dwelling look like? Let's seek the Lord, that we can say with
David, "One thing have I asked of Jehovah, that will I seek after:
that I may dwell in the house of Jehovah all the days of my life,
To behold the beauty of Jehovah, And to inquire in his temple."

10380851R00070